The role of media literacy in the fight against fakes and disinformation in the media space of Uzbekistan

Author:

Nozim Boronov

© Nozim Boronov
The role of media literacy in the fight against fakes and disinformation in the media space of Uzbekistan
by: Nozim Boronov
Edition: October '2024
Publisher:
Taemeer Publications LLC (Michigan, USA / Hyderabad, India)

© **Nozim Boronov**

Book	:	The role of media literacy in the fight against fakes and disinformation in the media space of Uzbekistan
Author	:	Nozim Boronov
Publisher	:	Taemeer Publications
Year	:	'2024
Pages	:	130
Title Design	:	*Taemeer Web Design*

N. Boranov.

The role of media literacy in the fight against fakes and disinformation in the media space of Uzbekistan.

Monograph.

This monograph entitled "The role of media literacy in the fight against fake and disinformation in the media space of Uzbekistan" describes the theoretical foundations, philological aspects of media literacy, social impact characteristics of fake and disinformation, and dissemination technologies.

The monograph is intended for professors and teachers of the faculties of journalism and mass communications, students, and those interested and professionals working in the field.

Responsible editor:

Yakuta Mamatova, doctor of philology, professor

Reviewers:

Sanobar Jumanova - Doctor of Philology (PhD)

Nodira Zohitova - Doctor of Philology (PhD)

TABLE OF CONTENTS

Introduction ....

Chapter I. MEDIA LITERACY AND DISINFORMATION IN THE MEDIA SPACE
1.1. The essence and development directions of media literacy ...
1.2. The role of media literacy in combating fake news and disinformation ...
Conclusion for Chapter I ....

Chapter II. CLASSIFICATION OF FAKE NEWS AND DISINFORMATION
2.1. The roots, types, and social consequences of fake news ...
2.2. The social impact of disinformation ...
2.3. Technological factors in the spread of fake news and disinformation ...
Conclusion for Chapter II ....

Chapter III. MEDIA LITERACY AS A FACTOR IN COMBATING INFORMATION ATTACKS
3.1. Technologies for spreading extremist content on social networks ...
3.2. Social media as a key tool in preventing the spread of fake information ...
3.3. Fact-checking as an element of media literacy ...

Conclusion for Chapter III ....
Conclusion ....
Appendix ....
List of References ....

INTRODUCTION

The relevance of the topic is determined by the informatization processes in our society in the new information age, alongside traditional mass media (television, radio, print media), the emergence of new means of mass communication, namely mobile communication systems and computer networks (the Internet), and the instant, extensive dissemination of limitless information flows to a broad audience. Additionally, it is shaped by the quality of this information and its profound impact on our life choices and socio-political activities. With the unparalleled development of the internet in the 21st century, the world has effectively become "one step closer"[1]. News from one corner of the world now reaches the other in mere seconds. Media's influence on modern society's development continues to grow each year, shaping people's social and psychological understanding and evaluation of their environment. The main features of contemporary media are "creativity and innovation"[2].

However, it has become increasingly common to encounter incorrect and harmful information within the news published in mass media and on official news websites. False, fabricated, and misleading information negatively influences the audience's mindset, disrupting relationships between people, undermining existing rules,

---

[1] Лебедева Е.Г. Фейковые новости как инструмент манипулятивного воздействия в медиасреде // Universum: филология и искусствоведение :электрон. научн. журн. 2021. 3(81). URL: https://7universum.com/ru/philology/archive/item/

[2] Муратова Н., Тошпулатова Н., Алимова Г. Fake news: медиада дезинформация [Матн]: қўлланма /.. – Ташкент: "Innovatsion rivojlanish nashriyot-matbaa uyi", 2020. – Б.10.

values, and traditions within society. As a result, fake news—what experts refer to as "disinformation"—has become one of modern journalism's most pressing issues[3]. "Fake news" is not merely a form of information but has evolved into a "new phenomenon of the 21st century", requiring both theoretical and practical investigation as a social issue[4].

The ability to distinguish accurate from inaccurate information is now expected not only from journalists but also from information consumers, as well as anyone who can process, disseminate, or create content. In this fast-paced informational environment, mass media must help equip consumers with the skills to objectively analyze and decide whether to accept or reject any given information, enabling them to avoid fake and even harmful information in this globalized world. As scholar Khurshid Dostmuhammad puts it, we need to cultivate an "information culture" or "info ethics"[5]—which has now become a matter of survival. Indeed, as Nobel laureate economist Herbert A. Simon noted, "Nowadays, information is devouring and consuming its recipients". "The issue today is not a shortage of information, but an

---

[3] Муратова Н., Тошпулатова Н., Алимова Г. Fake news: медиада дезинформация [Матн]: қўлланма /.. – Ташкент: "Innovatsion rivojlanish nashriyot-matbaa uyi", 2020. – Б.4.

[4] Муратова Н., Тошпулатова Н., Алимова Г. Fake news: медиада дезинформация [Матн]: қўлланма /.. – Ташкент: "Innovatsion rivojlanish nashriyot-matbaa uyi", 2020. – Б.12.

[5] Дўстмуҳаммад Х. Ахборот мўъжиза, жозиба, фалсафа, Т.: "Янги аср авлоди" 2013.Б. 317, Б. 44.

overwhelming abundance of it. Therefore, possessing the ability to seek out necessary information and assess its authenticity has become critically important".

New methods and skills for handling information were already developed in the 1960s and 1970s, leading to the establishment of what became known as the media education field. Following UNESCO recommendations, media education has been implemented in many developed countries worldwide. Its goal is to promote media literacy. The term "media literacy" merges two concepts: media literacy and information literacy. Information literacy refers to the set of skills and abilities for selecting, evaluating, processing, and transmitting information. Media literacy, in turn, refers to the set of skills and abilities needed to comprehend and evaluate the functioning of mass media.

From this perspective, this monograph will explore the theoretical foundations of media literacy, its philological aspects, the social impact characteristics of fake news and disinformation, their dissemination technologies, and the methodological foundations for defending against them within Uzbekistan's media landscape.

CHAPTER I. MEDIA LITERACY AND DISINFORMATION IN THE MEDIA SPACE

1.1. The essence and directions of development of media literacy

The modern world in which we live cannot be imagined without mass media. Media includes print, press, television, cinematography, radio, sound recording and the Internet. In recent years, media has taken a central place in people's lives. Media are divided into non-electronic print media and electronic media. Non-electronic printed media are "periodicals, newspapers and magazines, books, comics; Electronic media are radio, movies, television, computer (SD-ROM, USB), video games, Internet, recorded music, mobile phone, e-books"[6]. Sociologists say that, on average, "a civilized person" lives 75 years, spends about 50 years actively without sleep, and spends about 9 years watching TV"[7]. In the current era of globalization, it is impossible to sort all available information and deliver to the audience. Mass media, the Internet and its countless social sites, and the film industry constantly transmit a wide range and large amount of different information. Today, there is an extremely wide and diverse collection of information materials, content and resources, especially on the Internet, varying in accuracy, reliability and value. In addition, this information is available in various forms (text, image, statistical data, electronic or printed form) and can be obtained through online databases, portals, virtual and real libraries, document collections, databases, archives, museums, etc. The truthfulness and impartiality of the information depend on the reliability of the information source transmitting it. A source of information is usually a person or a carrier who has information of social importance (that is, of interest and need to the general public). So, which sources can be truthful and unbiased? When evaluating the source of information, first of all, it is necessary to determine the purpose for which the person receives the information. Sources of information are mainly traditional (official sources, i.e. documents, media materials, government decisions, life itself, etc.) and non-traditional (hotlines, social health centers, secondary raw materials, bottle reception, car washes and gas stations,

---

[6] Намазов Б., Файзиева М., Шарофаддинов Ш. Медиа ва ахборот саводхонлиги Ўқув қўлланма Тузувчилар:.. 17 б.

[7] Kubey, R. (1998). Obstacles to the Development of Media Education in the United States. Journal of Communication (Winter), pp.58-69.

markets and etc.) are divided into types. What type of information source is the most reliable, and which sources can be unbiased, neutral, transparent and quality-controlled? Researchers divide available sources of information into three categories: **primary**, **secondary**, and **tertiary**. **Primary sources** - original sources that do not interpret information. These may be research reports, price lists, speech texts, electronic communications, original artwork, manuscripts, photographs, diaries, personal letters, oral histories/interviews, or diplomatic documents. In most cases and in certain situations, it is recommended to use primary sources of information whenever possible. **Secondary sources** are considered as information provider. In this case, the information may be modified, analyzed or summarized (for example, in scientific books, journals, critical analysis or data interpretation). Recommended primary sources do not always contain more authoritative or unbiased information than secondary sources. Situations of subjective assessment of information can be eliminated by using verified secondary sources. A secondary source can be defined based on a specific field or a specific situation. **Tertiary sources** - sources that are organized and incorporate information from primary and secondary sources (for example, abstracts, bibliography, various manuals, encyclopedias, indexes, chronological tables, databases, etc.). It is an important skill to know how to choose the most useful for ourselves from all the information that the world offers us now and to use correctly and effectively. In this regard, the development of the current era requires any information consumer to be a special, unique literate in terms of information. A person who wants to be literate and competent in this regard must have a good understanding of information and information literacy. The term "information" has many definitions and can mean data, knowledge gained through research, experience or learning, as well as signals or signs. Simply said, information is information that has been collected, processed, and interpreted in a user-friendly form. Another different description of information is "knowledge presented in an easy to understand form". Information is derived from the Latin language, "information" means explanation, statement. In the past, behind this concept was understood the information given by people to each other orally, in writing and in other ways. Information in a broad sense is defined in the science of cybernetics. According to its founder, Norbert Wiener, "information is a description of content from the outside world, which we adapt to it and it to our feelings"[8]. The concept of information has been given different definitions by many scientists: Information is a concept that "changes us"[9]. Information is a concept that "reaches the mind of a person and increases his knowledge"[10]. "Information is a form that is meaningful to those who receive it and has actual or potential value for current or subsequent actions or decisions"[11]. On the other hand, the term "information" is "also used in the sense of giving information, transmitting information and disseminating it"[12]. What is media? Some researchers mean the mass

---

[8] Намазов Б., Файзиева М., Джалилов Ғ. Baktria Медиа ва ахборот саводхонлиги Педагоглар учун методик қўлланма. press Тошкент – 2018. - Б.43.

[9] Стэффорд Бир. Мозг Фирмы. М.: Радио и связь, 1993. — С. 16 .

[10] Blokdjik and Blokdjik, 1987 http://unesco.mil-for-teachers.unaoc.org/

[11] Davis and Olsen. Управленческие информационные системы: концептуальные основы, структура и развитие, 2-е издание, Нью-Йорк: McGraw-Hill. 1984

[12] Намазов Б., Файзиева М., Джалилов Ғ. Baktria Медиа ва ахборот саводхонлиги Педагоглар учун методик қўлланма. press Тошкент – 2018. - Б.43

media mainly. Others interpret mass media as an integral part of public communication[13]. Along with the concept of mass media, there is also a term such as **Mass Media** in modern society. The word "media" itself refers to a certain tool that transforms experience into knowledge, and its plural form "media" refers to signs that give meaning to the events of everyday life and implies the existence of many sign systems. The term "media" is very general, meaning any means of communication that conveys or "mediates" meaning. The telephone, radio, film, television, print, and the human voice, along with visual arts and sculpture, are all called "media." In the second half of the 20th century, all the mass media in the world consisted of news satellites, color television, cable television, cassettes, videotapes, VCRs, laser technology, electronic high-speed printing equipment, various generating and teaching machines, databases, the Internet and other network systems united into a universal system. All these media are constantly making new connections with each other and with the old media, i.e. press, radio, film, telephone, etc. By the late 1980s, the media space was further expanded by the field of video culture. In addition to television, press, radio, and the Internet, it is also used for storage and playback devices for print, film, audio, and video data, and other means of transmitting communicative symbols. In other words, media combines mass media and mass communication tools. Many researchers believe that the main feature of the situation in the global media space today is its unpredictability, the rapid pace of technological innovation. They believe that since the end of the 20th century, the priority among mass media has shifted to electronic mass media, that is, television and the Internet. Media, on the one hand, reflects reality, which is a product of a certain socio-

---

[13] Хлызова Н.Ю. Средства массовой информации и средства массовой коммуникации как сновные понятия медиаобразования/ Под ред. Л.П. Громовой. [Текст]/ СПб., 2008. – С.290.

cultural technological environment, on the other hand, it can seriously change it, create new standards, stereotypes, motives, behavior and lifestyle. In this sense, mass media has great potential and opportunities to influence society. The term "media" (Latin - medium, i.e. tool, mediator, method) refers to various forms of communication and information means. The concept of media includes the means of creating, copying, and distributing information, as well as technical means of information exchange between authors and mass audiences. Today, the term media is used as a synonym for media or mass media concepts. In building a democratic society and in the development of a country, ownership of information is as important as life. Citizens have the right to freedom of speech and access to social information. Media and other providers of information (library, archive, Internet, etc.) help ensure the right of every citizen to freely use information[14]. "Researchers include creativity (creativity, creativity) and innovation in the main aspects of modern media. Such a description of this term can be found at www.edu.jobsmarket.ru website[15]. "Media - mass media are communication channels that perform numerous and diverse functions aimed at distributing news, information and advertising information, recommending entertainment offers for both a wide and special audience"[16]. Media, as an important part of the communication system of any society, provides an opportunity to work together with non-media information sources, including libraries, archives, Internet providers and other information

---

[14] Медиа ва ахборот саводхонлиги Педагоглар учун методик қўлланма Тузувчилар: Б. Намазов, М. Файзиева, Ғ. Джалилов. Baktria press Тошкент – 2018. - 43б

[15] Медиа ва ахборот саводхонлиги Ўқув қўлланма Тузувчилар: Б. Намазов, М. Файзиева, Ш. Шарофаддинов. Б.47.

[16] www/advesti.ru/glossary/desk/1952

organizations, as well as citizens who create personal content.

tasks: ***Modern media tools perform the following***

- works as an information and knowledge channel, through which citizens can communicate with each other and make decisions based on the received information;

- supports competent discussions among public figures;

- is the main source of information about the environment;

- a means by which the society can learn about itself and helps the citizen to form a sense of solidarity with the society;

-helping to establish transparency of public life and public control over the government, acting as an impartial observer of the activities of state bodies by identifying cases of corruption, irresponsible management, illegal actions of associations;

- serves as a vital driving force of the democratic process, a guarantor of fair and free elections;

- represents the representatives of one nation and inter-national culture and serves as a factor establishing cultural relations;

- appears as an independent fighter for rights and social partnership, respecting the values of pluralism.

Information has been the most necessary of the products consumed by mankind. The need for it has always been strong. The development of information technologies, especially the emergence of the Internet, has greatly increased the speed of information preparation and delivery, and has expanded the possibilities of receiving it to an unprecedented level. Therefore, finding out whether the information transmitted in this process is correct or incorrect has become a difficult problem to solve. That is why "modern means of communication are increasingly turning into sources of information that are not verified or spread based on rumors"[17]. Such information, consisting of lies, fabrications, and fake information, received the name "fake news" in journalism and became an integral part of the modern media space. Users of modern media cannot immediately distinguish between correct information and "fake news". Because of its attractive, interesting nature, it attracts the public with its creativity, sensationalism, and attention-grabbing compared to formal, stilted, dry, factual messages. The rise of fakes, on the one hand, has a negative impact on the professionalism of the mass media, and on the other hand, the media immunity and media literacy of information consumers. As a result of the development of the Internet and social media, every consumer of information simultaneously fulfills the role of information distributor and public journalist. With the movement of a finger, a person can spread a message of dubious origin to thousands of people and unknowingly become a link in a chain of deadly disinformation. Why is it important to fight fakes? Because it is proven by facts that they can represent a real threat to stability and security. For example, it is known that the genocide in Rwanda (1993) was triggered by a false news broadcast on local radio. In 2018, 25 people were arbitrarily killed by the masses in India due to fake photos distributed through the WhatsApp messenger. In such conditions, it is the duty of every state and the duty

---

[17] Комиссаров М. А. "Проблема распространения недостоверной информации в СМИ и социальных медиа"// Тезисы к выступлению на 20-й Центрально-Азиатской Конференции СМИ "Будущее журналистики". https://www.osce.org/representative-on-freedom-ofmedia.2022.С.123.

of every citizen to correctly assess the threat posed by fakes and to be able to counter it. In this regard, it will be useful to strictly comply with the requirements of the law, to remind the informants of their responsibility in this regard once again. Because "feeling the responsibility of disseminating information, thinking about the legal consequences in this regard and not forgetting responsibility is one of the main tasks facing a modern person"[18]. It should combat fakes by creating immunity in citizens against various information attacks and promoting media literacy in cooperation with information distributors. In general, "Fake news" is both a harm and a benefit to society. It is definitely harmful to people with low media immunity. They easily fall into the "reality of fakes". But it is difficult to mislead and deceive a person with developed media literacy. He has developed critical thinking, and therefore he rechecks all information, compares sources, analyzes and accepts opinions. That is, "fake news" increases media immunity in the representatives of this society. Factors that can combat "fake news" are "knowledge, media literacy, healthy skepticism and fact-checking"[19]. Nowadays, the million types of information and the fact that it is created and disseminated through various media, i.e. mass media, require society members to have an important feature, that is, to be literate in the use of information in the mass media. "Information literacy is a set of competencies needed to acquire, understand, evaluate, adapt, create,

---

[18] Dimax. «Фейк» хабарларга қарши курашиш нега муҳим?// "Terabayt.Uz" ахборот технологиялари сайти. 2022.12

[19] Муратова Н., Тошпулатова Н., Алимова Г.. Fake news: медиада дезинформация [Матн]: қўлланма.

– Ташкент: "Innovatsion rivojlanish nashriyot-matbaa uyi", 2020. – Б.95.

store and present information for decision-making and problem analysis"[20].

• Determining, analyzing and evaluating the quality of information, that is, its reliability and truthfulness;

• Organization, storage or archiving of information;
• Effective use of information without violating the copyrights of information creators, observing ethical norms;

• Creation of new knowledge and exchange with them"[21]

An information literate person should be able to think critically, analyze information and use it to express his opinion, be able to learn independently, participate in the state activities and democratic processes in society, be a citizen who is always aware of important events and be ready to be a master of his profession. Such people should know how to collect, use, process and organize information based on ethical rules and norms. Many researches are being carried out in order to clarify the essence of media literacy, to show its place in multi-network social activity, to determine its purpose, tasks, and conceptual foundations. Special attention is paid to studying the theoretical foundations of media literacy. Why is it necessary to develop media and information literacy skills, which occupy an important place in the world news space today? The quality of received information is an important factor in the development of media literacy, and it can be distinguished from "very

---

[20] Ўша манба

[21] Намазов Б., Файзиева М., Джалилов Ғ. Baktria Медиа ва ахборот саводхонлиги Педагоглар учун методик қўлланма. press Тошкент – 2018. - Б.44.

good" to "very bad"[22]. That is why it is one of the most important social tasks to teach everyone who has the opportunity to transmit a media product to use media materials, to analyze them impartially and correctly, to accept or not, to correctly sort and own them.

While information literacy emerged from curriculum and materials designed for library users, media literacy emerged from media and citizen research. Since 1974, information literacy has been emphasized as a concept essential to acquiring, evaluating, and creating and sharing information and knowledge through a variety of tools and channels. The concept of media literacy has entered our lives with the process of using computer materials, and implies the understanding, selection, and evaluation of information as a leading distributor and processor of information, and sometimes as a creator. In addition, the concepts of information communication technology (ICT) literacy and digital literacy are informed by computer science and information technology science, and focus on the use of certain digital devices, software and infrastructure. ICT literacy is often used as an effective tool for other types of literacy. In addition, digital literacy is used along with information literacy as an ability to effectively and critically own information and evaluate information in different formats. Digital literacy is becoming a key driver of digital literacy in governance, citizenship, and economic development. Digital literacy is also closely related to media literacy, as it helps to collaborate and work safely and ethically on social media. In this way, ICT or technological literacy is linked to the skills required to manage information and media content. Since mass media are mainly used by young people, forming MAS skills in them is one of the most important

---

[22] Намазов Б., Файзиева М., Джалилов Ғ. Baktria Медиа ва ахборот саводхонлиги Педагоглар учун методик қўлланма. press Тошкент – 2018. - Б.14.

tasks. According to the data, "96 percent of the world's youth communicate through social networks"[23] Because young people are more sensitive to news than other media users and often tend to blindly accept it without checking it. There are many examples of this. For example, at the end of 2016 and the beginning of 2017, "games" called "Sin'iy kit", "Razbudi menya v 4:20", "F57" caused a lot of noise and killed a lot of young people who were looking for dangerous adventures on the network. Attacks on schools in various Russian cities in 2018 are linked to the 1999 Columbine school murders in America. In this regard, the point of view was expressed through media channels that Russian schoolchildren performed their actions under the influence of the society of fans who idealized American teenagers named Eric and Dylan, who appeared on social networks at that time and became popular. "Since such tragedies have increased due to the negative ideas propagated through Internet networks, by the beginning of the 21st century, the problem of media literacy among young people began to be actively discussed by mass media experts and scientists"[24]. Therefore, in order to protect the young generation from such cyber threats, implementing MASS MEDIA in the educational system has become an important necessity at the level of state policy. It is known that since the 60s of the 20th century, in the pedagogy of the world's leading countries, a special direction of "media education" has been formed, which helps schoolchildren and students to

---

[23] Алимов Б. Ёшларнинг ижтимоий тармоклар орқали мамлакат имижини оширишдаги роли. // «Ёшлар инновацион фаоллигини оширишнинг долзарб вазифалари» мавзусидаги республика илмий-амалий коференцияси тўплами). Т., 2019. // https://beruniyalimov.uz/

[24] РепортажДаниилаТуровского//Медуза.2016.15августа.URL:https://meduza.io/feature/2016/08/15/zashifrovan oe-podpolie

better adapt to the world of media culture, master the language of mass media, analyze media texts, etc. By the 1990s, media education became a compulsory component of education in all secondary schools (grades 1 to 12) in Canada and Australia. The development of this direction was also supported by UNESCO. The importance and support of media education has been mentioned several times in UNESCO decisions and recommendations (UNESCO conferences in Grunwald, 1982; Toulouse, 1990; Paris, 1997; Vienna, 1999; Seville, 2002, etc.). According to UNESCO's 2002 recommendations, "media education is part of the basic right of every citizen to freedom of speech and information, which contributes to the support of democracy. Recognizing the differences in the approaches and development of media education in different countries, it is recommended to introduce it as much as possible within the framework of national curricula, as well as within the framework of additional, non-formal education and self-education throughout a person's life. Currently, in countries such as European countries, the USA, Australia and Russia, media education is included in the education system as a compulsory subject.

Media education can be divided into the following main areas:

1) Media education of future professionals in the world of press, radio, television, film, video and the Internet - journalists, editors, directors, producers, actors, cameramen, etc.;

2) Media education in the process of professional development of future teachers at universities and pedagogical institutes, university and school teachers in media culture courses;

3) As a part of general education, media education can be combined with traditional or autonomous (special,

optional, circle, etc.) subjects for pupils and students studying in ordinary schools, secondary special educational institutions, universities);

4) Media education in institutions of additional education and recreation centers (houses of culture, centers for extracurricular activities, centers for aesthetic and artistic education, clubs at the place of residence, courses, etc.);

5) Remote (online) media education of schoolchildren, students and adults using the press, television, radio, video, Internet system (media criticism plays a big role here);

6) Independent / continuous media education (theoretically, it can be carried out during a person's life).

MIL, i.e. full use of the benefits of media and information literacy, means that media and information literacy should be accepted as a whole and integrated in its content as competence (knowledge, skills and competences). Integrating media and information literacy into educational processes builds problem-solving and critical thinking skills in young learners. It also teaches analysis of primary sources, evaluation of information based on certain functions of social services considered mandatory for media and libraries, archives and other information services. Students should be able to understand and analyze how media content and other information is created, how to evaluate the information provided by these services, and be able to use media and information for different purposes. In addition, students should be able to analyze diversity and pluralism in the presentation of information in different media and information systems, as well as local and global media.

In the field of media and information literacy, young people must acquire the following skills:

- interactive skills (learns to communicate through media and try oneself in different media roles, express one's opinion and instructions);

- critical analysis skills (the ability to understand and interpret media content of various forms develops in students based on the ability to evaluate and interpret various media content and genres using analytical methods);

- aesthetic and creative skills (the student develops the ability to see, hear, understand, create and interpret media text or media content by creating media content);

- security skills (forms the ability to protect one's private territory in the virtual space, to get out of difficult situations and avoid them, to observe security and to avoid harmful content and communications).

Formation of media and information literacy requires the student to fully immerse himself in the process of media content production. Experimentation is an important learning step for media and information literacy education. It is important that learners have the opportunity to gain new experiences by trying out different roles as participants in the media production and distribution process. Therefore, ask the children, "What did I learn about the media during this exercise?" It is very important to learn to find the answer to the question. The best way to develop media and information literacy is to use a variety of media. However, in order to acquire these skills in young people, it is not enough to automatically use the media repeatedly. For this, we need a coach and mentor who can teach to fight for values, to think about the choice of a certain media resource, who can direct the reader to reliable information, and who can help with issues related to the popularity of the media. The teacher has a role in the process of media education. A teacher working with media should begin by thinking about his own relationship with media: How do I use media? How do they affect my work? A teacher doesn't need to be a technical genius or to know the degree to which media culture is formed in the hearts of young people, but he should be able to give advice based on his life experience on issues related to network etiquette. The qualification of a media literacy teacher is based on personal media skills, experience and interest in media, willingness to discuss various aspects of media literacy, and active participation in educational activities. A media literate teacher does not debate the correctness of learners' opinions or their media tastes, but rather uses them as a starting point for discussion. A media literacy teacher values young learners' experience even it is small; it provides students with enough information and skills to learn how to protect themselves from the harmful effects of the media. In modern society, the need to communicate more competently and safely with mass media is to learn to accept them correctly, to acquire communication skills not only with traditional print and electronic media, but also with all new technologies of mass, personal and computer communication, in the "media space" requires being able to move with confidence. In the modern world, media education is "the culture of communication with mass media, It is recognized as a process of personal development with the help and materials of mass media for the formation of creative, communicative abilities, critical thinking, skills of full perception, interpretation, analysis and evaluation of media texts, teaching various forms of self-expression using media techniques. Media education is not only pedagogy and art education, but also art studies (including film studies, literature studies, theater studies), cultural studies, history (world artistic culture and art history), psychology (art psychology), artistic perception, all existing creative fields, fields of humanities and etc. is also closely related. Media education, which meets the needs of modern pedagogy in personal development, expands the methods and forms of training with students and pupils. A comprehensive study of the virtual world of the computer, which synthesizes the features of the press, film, television, video, Internet, almost all traditional media, will correct the one-sided, isolated important shortcomings of the traditional art education, literature, music or painting, analysis of a particular work visual means of expression and they help to separate the content. Media education is the conduct of classes based on problematic, heuristic, game and various other effective forms of education that develop the student's individuality, independence of thinking, direct involvement in creative activities, perception, interpretation and analysis of the structure of media text, and the acquisition of knowledge about media culture. it also opens up endless possibilities. By combining lectures and hands-on activities, media education introduces students to the process of creating media cultural works, bringing the audience into the internal laboratory of the main media professions, which can be done both autonomously and through the inclusion of traditional academic subjects in the media process. In order for schoolchildren and students to become media literate, they should learn not only how some mass media texts are structured, but also how these texts express various political, ideological, economic, socio-cultural interests. Today, within the framework of the project "Promoting stability and peace in Central Asia" implemented with the financial support of the European Union, "Three points"[25] - an information campaign on increasing literacy in mass media is organized and supported. Poor quality or false and misleading information creates false perceptions of the world.

---

[25] Королева О. Сиз нима учун медиа саводли бўлишингиз керак? (Курбонбоева Ш. Таржимаси)// https://newreporter.org/uz/author/shahnoza/2022.

1.2. The role of media literacy in combating fake and disinformation

1. The teaching and learning process of MASS equips educators with a wide range of knowledge to pass on their knowledge to the next generation. 2. MAS provides important knowledge about the functioning of media and information channels in a democratic society, provides an understanding of the conditions necessary to evaluate the activities of media and information services within the scope of their functions and to implement these functions and develop basic skills. 3. A society with media and information literacy encourages the development of free, independent and diverse media and open information systems.

MASS itself consists of several components[26]:

Component 1. Possession. Determining the need for the ability to search, own and extract information and media content (component 1 - ownership). The first component of MASS is understood as the ability to implement, obtain and maintain ownership of information and media content using appropriate technologies. It includes the ability to identify information, media content, and knowledge needs and to identify useful information and media content from all sources and formats, including print, audio, visual, and digital, to meet those needs. Information can be extracted and stored electronically from libraries, museums, personal documents, and any other source.

Component 2. Evaluation. Understanding, analyzing and evaluating information and media

---

[26] Медиа ва ахборот саводхонлиги Педагоглар учун методик қўлланма Тузувчилар: Б. Намазов, М. Файзиева, Ғ. Джалилов. - Baktria press Тошкент – 2018. – Б.46.

(component 2 — evaluation). The second component of MAS is defined as the ability to understand, critically analyze and evaluate the activities and functions of information, media content, media and information delivery organizations in the context of universal human rights and fundamental freedoms. It includes comparing facts, distinguishing facts from assumptions according to timing (new/outdated), understanding underlying ideologies and values, and identifying how social, economic, political, professional, and technological forces shape media and information content. It also includes assessment of information quality (accuracy, relevance, authenticity, truthfulness and completeness). Moreover, in today's era of information overload, people need to master technical skills such as organizing, selecting and synthesizing media and information. It is important to understand the nature of the functions and behavior of media institutions, media professionals, and information providers, and to know how to analyze information and media messages. It is important to understand the importance of media and information in a broader context, including for promoting freedom of expression, freedom of information and ownership of information. It also helps to understand the relationship and impact of MASS on altruism, democracy and governance. Media and information literate people recognize the economic, social and political power and control of media companies and news providers and social organizations. Since the MASS hidden feature is a broad concept, its levels should be presented in profile view rather than as separate sets. It is important to emphasize that a person can show high results on some indicators and low results on others. For example, a person may perform well in activities related to evaluating and understanding the functions of media and information providers (Component 2), while the opposite may be seen in extracting and owning media and information (Component 1), especially the use of information appears only in cases where it is required to be done via a computer or the Internet. On the other hand, a person's performance on the 3rd component of the MASS is related to the performance of the other two components. Effectively organized media education, the MASS process teaches how to counter various negative influence methods that serve to shape public opinion, such as disinformation, lobbying, manipulation, and propaganda. Knowing the essence of these main ideological weapons in information warfare in virtual space is of great practical importance. On the other hand, a person's performance on the 3rd component of the MASS is related to the performance of the other two components. Effectively organized media education, the MASS process teaches how to counter various negative influence methods that serve to shape public opinion, such as disinformation, lobbying, manipulation, and propaganda. Knowing the essence of these main ideological weapons in information warfare in virtual space is of great practical importance.

Lobbying (from the English lobby - a closed walking area, a corridor) is a set of various methods and methods of influencing the decision-making structure to achieve a specific goal. In 1864 in America, the meaning of this word acquired a political meaning. The term "lobbying" came to mean buying votes for money in the corridors of Congress.

Manipulation is a method of psychological influence, which, on the one hand, consists in changing the direction of activity carried out imperceptibly for people; on the other hand, it is a type of exercise of power in which those who possess it influence the behavior of others without revealing the nature of the behavior that influences it.

Propaganda (Latin propaganda - to be spread) is an activity that popularizes and spreads ideas in the public mind (verbally or with the help of mass media). The essence of propaganda is that under its influence, each person behaves in the same way as his behavior.Thus, after analyzing the goals, tasks and methods of information warfare, the traditional struggle to acquire material values in the developing information society will change and move more to the information field, which will naturally lead to the increase of information warfare.

The development of information warfare was related to the new, more effective and mass distribution of media and information delivery tools that existed before. Media literacy helps a person to actively use the opportunities of television, radio, video, film, press, Internet information sphere, to better understand the language of media culture. The basis of modern media education is the problems and tasks of developing a person through the means and material of mass communications. Media education, media literacy serves as a basis for forming a new personal culture. Effectively organized media classes help preserve traditional forms of education and upbringing, adapt them to the new information environment, and help young people find new opportunities for self-realization in a rapidly changing world. On June 9-10, 2022, the first International Conference on Media Literacy was held in Almaty. During the two-day event, media literacy experts from Kazakhstan, Uzbekistan and Tajikistan discussed ideas for improving media and information literacy (MASS) in the Central Asian region. The main idea of media literacy in the conference is to have critical thinking that allows you to filter information, which remains the same in all countries of the world. However, each country in different regions has its own characteristics of mentality, legislation, and people's preferences that affect the success of MASS promotion. Therefore, the need for separate national strategies was emphasized. It was specially recognized that many innovative projects are being implemented in the countries of the Central Asian region - Kazakhstan, Tajikistan and Uzbekistan to support the improvement of media and information literacy and that all parties will be interested in media literacy strategies.

Media literacy is not about ideology or politics, but about the ability to decode messages and critically perceive information. "Critical thinking is a vital skill that all citizens, young and old, must acquire as active participants in a democratic society. It is a favorable space for ensuring stability and solving social issues. It also provides a bridge between the government and citizens, transparency and accountability of activities," [27] said Lawrence Hardy, director of USAID's regional mission in Central Asia. Society's resistance to fakes and disinformation during the crisis was hotly discussed as another important topic of the International Conference. The organization and holding of such an international event is another proof that the problem of fake news is really global.

Media performs a variety of functions, including:

- works as a channel of information and knowledge, through these channels citizens can communicate with each other and make decisions based on the received information;

- conducting competent discussions between public figures supports;

- beyond our direct experience, is the main source of information about the environment;

- a community in which society can know about itself and a citizen which helps in forming a sense of solidarity with is a tool;

- transparency of public life and public over government helping to establish control, corruption, irresponsibility determination of cases of illegal actions of management, associations an impartial observer of the activities of state bodies through;

---

[27] Медиа саводхонлик бўйича халқаро конференцияда МАСни тарғиб қилишнинг миллий стратегиялари таклиф қилинди | Янги репортер (newreporter.org)

- the vital driving force of the democratic process, honest and serves as a guarantor of free elections;

- a factor that represents inter-national culture and establishes cultural ties, as well as between representatives of the same nation serves;

- law and social, respecting the values of pluralism appears as an independent fighter for partnership[28].

Conclusions on chapter I:

In conclusion, it can be said that it is difficult to imagine the modern world without mass media. Their use inevitably requires the formation of media literacy and, in a broader sense, the culture of information exchange. Media literacy helps a person to actively use the possibilities of television, radio, video, film, press, Internet information sphere, to better understand the language of media culture. Modern youth need a new type of relationship with the information environment, which has formed a world of values outside of the usual educational sphere, developed ethno-cultural experience and values. In this sense, the role of the school and the teacher is increasing dramatically. The basis of modern media education is the problems and tasks of developing a person through the means and material of mass communications. Media education, media literacy serves as a basis for forming a new personal culture. Effectively organized media classes help preserve traditional forms of education and upbringing, adapt them to the new information environment, and help young people find new

---

[28] Медиа ва ахборот саводхонлиги Ўқув қўлланма Тузувчилар: Б. Намазов, М. Файзиева, Ш. Шарофаддинов. - Baktria press Тошкент – 2018. – Б. 28

opportunities for self-realization in a rapidly changing world.

CHAPTER II. CLASSIFICATION OF FAKE AND DISINFORMATION

2.1. The roots, types and social consequences of fake news

Media literacy teaches you to distinguish fake news from real ones. In order to distinguish a real fact from a "fake", first of all, it is necessary to have a critical approach to information, to analyze the received information, to compare it with other sources, and to be able to draw independent conclusions about it. Conclusions must be based on good faith, experience and knowledge. "Fake news" poses a great danger in any country and society. Today, the words "fake" and "fake news" have been used as terms in the recent past, but the history of spreading false information goes back a long way. When it comes to the history of the emergence of the concept of "fake news", there is information that its roots go back to ancient times. For example, in the first century BC, "Octavian leads a campaign of disinformation against his rival Mark Antony. She spreads rumors that Mark has become an alcoholic and has become a puppet of Queen Cleopatra VII of Egypt.[29]" There are many such examples from history. Fake, false information, which today is generally called "fake news" and which, if it is not studied, analyzed and prevented in the information world, will cause huge negative consequences and cause heated debates, was first communicated in the form of rumors

---

[29] Kaminska, Izabella (January 17, 2017). "A lesson in fake news from the info-wars of ancient Rome". Financial Times. Financial Times. Retrieved July 4, 2017.

before the emergence of journalism. common among people. In the development of oral communication, such information was used for various conflicts and interests. The oral appearance of false, fabricated information in conversation has been preserved even now, and its influence is no less than that of modern "fakes". So who benefits from creating fake news and why? First of all, fake news is created to distract the general public from really important news. Because the main purpose of fake news distribution is to influence public opinion, they are usually supported mainly by politicians. When comparing the mass media, it becomes clear that the modern term "fake news" appeared recently. They were especially popular in 2016-2017. In particular, this phrase has been actively used in all media since the last presidential campaign in America in 2016. In 2017, Britain's Collins English Dictionary named "fake news" as its phrase of the year. The phenomenon of fake news was first studied by the American journalist Cheryl Atkinson[30], who, as part of her work, encountered a large amount of false information distributed in connection with the election campaign of Donald Trump and Hillary Clinton in the United States. During the campaign for the next presidential election in the United States, there were many scandals surrounding the candidate Donald Trump. In order to divert attention from the publication of new interesting facts from the life of the businessman, the candidate for the position of national security adviser Michael Flynn publishes a post on social media about the activities of the Democrats under the sensational title "Sex crimes with children", thus he increasingly focuses the public's attention on the members of the Democratic Party. focuses on the ongoing scandal, and Trump's moral image will no longer appear so negative. Later it turns out that this message is fake.

---

[30] Attkisson Sharyl. The Smear: How Shady Political Operatives and Fake News Control What You See, What You Think, and How You Vote. HarperCollins, 2017.

"Such "fake" information related to famous persons was also given about the death of Gulnara Karimova, the daughter of the first President of Uzbekistan, Islam Karimov, or the death of the President of Turkmenistan, Gurbanguly Berdimuhamedov. But soon it became known that these reports were "fake"[31]. Another example: in Syria, news under the term "fake news" was widely used to organize the process of manipulation. Subjects of manipulation drew people's attention and controlled their views in accepting reality based on their own interests. Accordingly, the lies spread in Syria are: "1) complete lies (absolute) - knowingly giving completely false information; 2) partially false - preparation of unfounded information with one lie that does not correspond to reality, among other correct sources; 3) a lie conveyed through silence (where the author knows the facts of the real event, but tries not to influence the audience with a certain image)[32]. Creating fake news on the Internet is also useful to increase popularity or income. When celebrity news breaks, fans are quick to spread the news and repost or comment. Thus, the resource becomes more popular and the profit from it increases. Fake news can also be created for the purpose of RR, for example, to gain popularity. Russian researcher A.P. Sukhodolov defines the concept of "fake news" as "stylistically created like real news, but completely or partially false news"[33]. S. N.

---

[31] Муратова Н. Fake news: медиада дезинформация [Матн]: қўлланма / Н. Муратова, Н. Тошпулатова, Г. Алимова. – Ташкент: "Innovatsion rivojlanish nashriyot-matbaa uyi", 2020. –Б.104.

[32] Ўша манба.

[33] Суходолов А.Феномен «Фейковых новостей» в современном медиапространстве // Евроазиатское сотрудничество: гуманитарные аспекты. 2017. №1. URL: https://cyberleninka.ru/article/n/fenomen-feykovyh-novostey-v-sovremennom-mediaprostranstve

Ilchenko in his work entitled "Fake in the Practice of Electronic Mass Media: Criteria of Credibility" recognizes that "a fake is a journalistic message published in the mass media containing unreliable and unverified information that does not correspond to actual facts and empirical reality."[34] All researchers say that the purpose of creating and spreading fakes is to influence the public mind, to instill certain ideas in the population. Fake news is aimed at changing public opinion about a political, social, entertainment, event, person or group of people, etc. can be divided into fakes. Fake news can also be created intentionally or unintentionally.

Researchers at the London School of Economics and Politics distinguish six categories of fake news[35]:

1. Foreign interference in local elections through fake news.

2. Spreading fake news based on advertising traffic for profit.

3. Parody and satire.

4. Low-quality journalism.

5. News that received a fake marker representing a different ideology.

6. News that question the traditional forms of power and power relations.

---

34 Ильченко С.Н. (2016). Фейк в практике электронных СМИ: критерии достоверности // Медиаскоп. № 4. http://www.mediascope.ru/2237 (дата обращения 23.02.2019)

35 Ўша маньба

A. P. Sukhodolov in his article "Fenomen "feikovyx novostey" v sovremennom media prostranstve" offers his classification of fake news based on the ratio of reliable and unreliable information. According to him, "fakes" are "totally false; fake news containing lies against the background of reliable information; may be fake news based on a real story with some details distorted. The researcher also distinguishes between "fake news" that reports on a real event that happened in the past and "news" that reports on a real event, but distorts the location of the action, depending on the reliability of the time and place conditions of the event. Depending on the composition of the persons mentioned in the "Fake news", the scientist "news" containing a link to the statement of the claimant published on behalf of the fake account; defines "news" that shows a secondary participant of the event as the main one and "news"[36] based on unconfirmed testimonies of persons who witnessed any events. Depending on the purpose of creation and distribution, it was created and distributed for the purpose of attracting the consumer, created and distributed for the purpose of obtaining political advantages, for the purpose of discrimination, for the purpose of increasing Internet traffic, for the purpose of fraudulently taking money and other property of consumers, for the purpose of damaging the information stored on the user's computer; In order to draw attention to a particular person, company, project or movement, "news" classifies "news" created and distributed in order to gain certain advantages in market management or economic activity[37]. Depending on the

---

[36] Ўша манба

[37] Суходолов А. П. Феномен «Фейковых новостей» в современном медиапространстве // Евроазиатское сотрудничество: гуманитарные аспекты. 2017. №1. URL: https://cyberleninka.ru/article/n/fenomen-feykovyh-novostey-v-sovremennom-mediaprostranstve

level of perception of authenticity, fakes are, in the opinion of the author, clearly fake "news", "news" that raises doubts about the reliability and prompts consumers to verify the information received; can appear as "news" that is reliably forged, but whose authenticity is almost beyond doubt.

N	Types of Fake news	Practical examples
1	**Clickbait:** sensational headlines designed to get clicks and shares, often leading to misleading or false articles.	
2	**Propaganda:** Dissemination of false or misleading information with the intent to influence public opinion or behavior.	
3	**Conspiracy theories:** baseless claims that a powerful group or organization is secretly controlling events and manipulating societal structures.	
4	**Satire:** Humorous content that is not meant to be taken seriously, but can be misleading if not interpreted as satire.	

| 5 | **Information out of context:** Using a quote or information out of context to support a false narrative. |  |

In conclusion, all researchers say that the purpose of creating and spreading fakes is to influence the public mind, to impose certain ideas on the population. Fake news can also be created intentionally or unintentionally. Trend micro companies recognize that the spread of fakes on social networks is a business that can make good money. It is also possible to use bots and paid teams of real users to create fake content.

2.2. The Social impact of disinformation

News has been of interest to people of all ages. People are interested in knowing what is happening in their city, country and abroad. Despondent viewers watch news coverage of any major event or cry while reading or hearing news coverage of events that have occurred. But also the material published and reprinted in the worldwide "cobweb" turns out to be fabricated lies, purposefully woven into sorbets. Such news reports are difficult to identify among the strong flow of information, because it is no coincidence that they appear in the modern media space. With their help, information necessary for authors is actively promoted and public opinion is formed. Although many countries have already started an active fight against "fakes", the threat of their increase in number remains open on the information agenda [38]. Fake

---

[38] Фейковые новости в медиапространстве – материал взят с сайта Студворк https://studwork.org/shop/219495-feykovye-novosti-

information threatens the life and (or) health of citizens, mass violation of public order and (or) public safety. Fake news is always spread for a specific purpose, namely to shape public opinion about an event, person or group of people. Any fake can be verified for authenticity, but people ignore it because they believe they can tell the truth from the fake. In addition, people lack information literacy, don't want to spend time confirming or denying information, and in some cases want to believe the information they see in front of them [39]". Although social networks, especially Facebook and Twitter, actively implement algorithms to combat fake news, their work is not always successful. Human nature is prone to "fake", disinformation, that is, to exaggerate or, on the contrary, make something smaller. Today, as a result of technological progress, it is easier to reflect this tendency in real life. The time and space-free possibilities of the Internet have started to serve its rapid and wide spread. Canadian philosopher Herbert Marshall McLuhan, one of the foremost researchers of the influence of information on the public mind, argued that mass media are "natural resources[40]". In today's modern world, the struggle for information resources has come to the fore. Understanding the nature of "fake" news based on rumors helps to clearly define the concepts of "fake" and "disinformation". Information is often characterized by the concepts of truth/false and reliability. Information is true if it corresponds to reality. Truth is represented by the correct

---

v-media-prostranstvehttps://studwork.org/shop/219495-feykovye-novosti-v-media-prostranstve.

[39] Маматова Я., Сулайманова С.Ўзбекистон медиатаълим тараққиёти йўлида. Ўқув қўлланма.–Т.: «Extremum-press», 2015. – Б. 94

[40] Ўша манба

presentation of fact[41]. So, a fact is a verified, reliable statement of reality. Disinformation as a type of information creates a false picture of reality in the audience. "Complete or partial distortion of facts, concealment of information, incorrect emphasis on the message in communication, etc. are disinformation tools"[42]. Currently, many researchers are focusing their attention on aspects that allow us to distinguish fake news from real ones. Fakes, by their very nature, consist of false information with elements of verisimilitude and credibility, a common feature that distinguishes them from disinformation and is necessary for it. S.N. As Ilchenko rightly noted, "the more unbelievable and unbelievably fake a fake is, the more likely it is to spread in the media"[43]. What is the difference between fake and classic disinformation, which has a long history as an integral element of almost all forms of mass mind manipulation since ancient times? First, disinformation is based on a combination of truth, half-truths, and lies. "The element of credibility, the apparent credibility of the message, is imperative. This is not required for a fake. The more fake information resembles the truth, the more effective it is at influencing the public mind"[44]. Second, disinformation spans the space of various journalistic genres. It can be a

---

[41] ClaireWardle, Hossein Derakhshan, "Information Disorder. Toward an interdisciplinary f ramework for research and policymaking", Council of Europe, 2017. Б.45. - ii боб. Fake news бугун.

[42] Маматова Я., Сулайманова С.Ўзбекистон медиатаълим тараққиёти йўлида. Ўқув қўлланма.–Т.: «Extremum-press», 2015. – Б. 94.

[43] Ильченко С. Н. Как нас обманывают СМИ: манипуляция информацией. СПб.: Питер, 2019. 38 б

[44] Воронова О.Е. Трушин А.С. .Функции фейков в современных информационных войнах.// https://histrf.ru/magazine/article/

report, an interview, an article, or even a journalistic inquiry.

Unlike disinformation, fake news has a "shell" of its own genre - a special type of news that creates an imaginary, non-real-life type of information. At the same time, a flashy headline is a hallmark of a fake as a news phenomenon. Third, disinformation may not differ in the relevance of the information it affects immediately; and the fake, of course, carries a sensational, sensational message that shocks everyone. "It is the desire for sensationalism and exclusivity - the result of the growing competition of media and Internet resources - that some experts believe is the main reason for the rapid spread of fake news content, which has reached an alarming scale."

Fourth, misinformation, even in rare cases, can be unintentional, due to error, oversight, or professional dishonesty on the part of the informant. A fake is always the result of deliberate distortion of the real situation, falsification, deliberate and provocative distortion of false facts. "Fakes do not appear spontaneously, but are formed in the context of the confrontation between the country and the Western powers, to solve political, military and economic problems, and with some purpose."[45]

Sixth, disinformation can exist covertly and "operate" for a long time. And as quickly as a fake appears in the information space at a well-defined time, it can disappear from the current agenda in the same way. Seventh, unlike disinformation, the mechanism of spreading fake news has its own characteristics. "Fakes spread like a 'virus' in society due to their 'emotional contagion' effect. In fact, the whole secret of the effectiveness of "fake news" is the resonant nature of the

---

[45] Ильченко С. Н. Как нас обманывают СМИ: манипуляция информацией. СПб.:Питер, 2019. С. 295.

information in the fake and viral mechanism of its distribution."⁴⁶.

Eighth, disinformation and fakes differ in their genesis. According to its origin, disinformation goes back to the art and methods of military tactics ("military deception") adopted in order to mask the real political goals and intentions in diplomatic activities. "The origin of the fake is related to the products of mass (daily) consciousness and mass (mass) culture, such as rumors, practical jokes ... microgens of political humor (sketch, anecdote). That's why it's no coincidence that experts distinguish comic news or "news that hasn't happened yet" in the flow of fake information."⁴⁷.

In particular, political fakes are often distributed to morally justify the aggressive actions of the United States in front of the world public opinion. To this end, in order to justify the bombing of Yugoslavia in the late 1990s, the influential Ci-en-en channel deliberately created an "enemy image" in the minds of the public and spread fake information that "700 Albanian children were used to create a blood bank for Serbian soldiers."⁴⁸.

Such global political "fakemakers" quote Goebbels, the Propaganda Minister of the Third Reich, "In order for

---

[46] Манойло А. В. «Фейковые новости» как метод перехвата информационной повестки в условиях современного информационного противоборства // Культурная политика. 2019. № 1. Официальный сайт «История.рф». С. 4. URL: https://histrf.ru/magazine/release

[47] Ўша манба

[48] Серов А. Дезинформация как инструмент внешней политики ряда зарубежных стран // Зарубежное военное обозрение. 2019. № 8.- С. 16.

them to believe a lie, it has to be terrible."[49] It is no exaggeration to say that they have mastered the guide well.

Scientists at the University of Pennsylvania analyzed countless examples of fake news and divided them into seven main categories. An article entitled "Feykovye novosti — eto ne prosto lojnaya informatsiya: concept explikatsi i taxonomy online content" was published in the "American Behavioral Scientist" magazine. The authors of this article describe the following fake news as "newspaper ducks, preconceived opinion, satire, disinformation, commentary, advisory (persuasive) information, and urban journalism." [50] identified such types as Scientists have compared this type of material with real reliable news.

They found that there are certain characteristics that distinguish reliable material from false information. Fake news usually doesn't follow a journalistic style, it's less consistent and offers people emotional feedback instead of more facts. Also, obscene or provocative headlines, lack of sources of information, or links to an "anonymous source" are signs of fake news. According to M. Molina, one of the authors of the article, identifying the characteristics of different forms of real and fake online news will not only help people distinguish fakes, but this data will also be useful in creating artificial intelligence systems that will automatically warn people about possible disinformation.

Shiyam Sundar, another co-author of the study, notes that "acknowledging the diversity of online news is important to correct the expectations of readers and some public figures who accuse the media of falsifying information. nn of information has also led to the

---

[49] Воронова О.Е. Трушин А. С. .Функции фейков в современных информационных войнах.// https://histrf.ru/magazine/article/

[50] Ўша манба

widespread spread of visual fakes"[51]. There are two types of visual fakes: photo fakes and video fakes. Photofakes as an effective means of manipulating world public opinion left a significant mark during the Ukrainian events of 2014. For example, one of the photos showed a long line of people with emaciated children. According to the article, Crimean residents fleeing from "aggressive Russia" were placed in holiday homes in the Ukrainian city of Kherson. In fact, it was a photograph from the late 1990s of Macedonian refugees fleeing the threat of ethnic cleansing by Kosovo Albanians.

The widespread use of digital manipulation has led to the emergence of a new technology called deepfake. According to the researchers, artificial intelligence-based synthesis of fake but completely reliable photo and video content can lead to serious threats. "Deep fake technologies are subjects, special services of many foreign countries; terrorist and extremist organizations; political parties; It is required by PR and advertising agenciesDeep fakes can also be used in the interests of information warfare, criminal activity, moral discrediting of unpopular politicians, and the overthrow of political regimes. Representing a new type of information threat, "deep fakes" can be used by Western politicians to falsify information to justify political decisions that are beneficial to themAt the VI Congress of World News Agencies held in Sofia in June 2019, the President of Bulgaria R. Radev rightly stated that "fake news in the era of widespread digital technologies can cause more damage than bullets and missiles." Video fakes, like photo fakes, pose a great threat to the world community today. The technology of fake video imitations has been tested several times in Syria. The practice of using videos as a means of fake information about the situation in Syria poses serious military and political threats. Terrorists use such fake

---

[51] Воронова О.Е. Трушин А. С. .Функции фейков в современных информационных войнах.// https://histrf.ru/magazine/article/

videos to misinform the world community.

The lack of international legal norms that allow video provocateurs to escape responsibility is a serious problem that needs to be addressed unconditionally. Western countries are the authors of the project of video plots called "White Helmets". In general, fakes perform many tasks (functions). Russian researchers M.O. Voronova and A.S. Trushin notes that "fakes are used not only as a means of imitating a non-existent event, but also as a means of inciting inadequate military and political decisions." Until they find out. fakes "also perform the functions of disinforming the audience, promoting certain political positions, causing panic, intimidation, and misleading to attack the current government." A.V. According to Monoylo, "they can be used to divert the attention of the mass audience from real and political problems and to change their opinion, to weaken or, on the contrary, to strengthen protest activity."[52].

The concept of "fake" has spread to other public spheres today. Fakes were also actively used as a tool of information warfare. Wide spread of fake information that misleads the public, causes "digital aggression" in the field of international relations, causes panic, casts a shadow on reputable political leaders, harms respectable corporations, causes havoc in the banking sector, and destabilizes the situation. world today has led to the emergence of a new type of professional activity - Fact-checking, that is, fact-checking. Its task is to fight against voluntary or involuntary fake producers, to check the facts, to verify the veracity of the information distributed in the mass media and on the Internet. Lisa Fazio,

---

[52] Манойло А. В. «Фейковые новости» как метод перехвата информационной повестки в условиях современного информационного противоборства // Культурная политика. 2019. № 1. Официальный сайт «История.рф». С. 4. URL: https://histrf.ru/magazine/release

associate professor of psychology and human development at Vanderbilt University, points out that "susceptibility to fake news is linked to people's cognitive and behavioral domains." Faccio and his colleagues have shown in an experiment that repetition of information increases the audience's level of trust in it. That is, the more often fake news is seen, the stronger a person believes in its authenticity.

Dr. Pedro Lind of the Institute for Computational Physics at the University of Stuttgart, along with his colleagues Luciano da Silva, Jose Andrade, and Hansom Errmann, studied the spread of rumors and gossip. Scientists determined the time of spread of certain rumors and the number of people who "consumed" them by means of test experiments conducted among students. In the model developed by the scientists, each student appeared as a node in the graphic system. Each node was connected to several others—each student's neighbors and friends—with whom they could share their data. They note that "as a person's number of friends increases, the time it takes to spread a rumor increases in a logarithmic progression, and eventually the circle of gossipers expands."[53].

According to Paul Lazarsfeld, Bernard Berelson, and Hazel Gods in The People's Choice, "the mass media first influence opinion leaders or leaders of certain groups, and then these people disseminate the information received to others."[54].

---

[53] Ўша манба

[54] Pedro G. Lind, Luciano R. da Silva, José S. Andrade, Jr., and Hans J. Herrmann. Phys. Rev. E 76, 036117 – Published 27 September 2007   URL https://proxylibrary.hse.ru:2291/pre/abstract/10.1103/PhysRevE.76.036117

Many researchers point out that fakes start from rumors and jokes[55]. In particular, S. S. Raspopova and Ye. N. Bogdan wrote it in "Fake news: the nature of origin"." The article defines fake news as "false, fabricated news material that can mislead the audience but is recognizable and verifiable." They consider rumors and jokes to be the prototype of fakes. Rumors and jokes refer to an anonymous primary source who is familiar with the situation and has a close family or friendly relationship with the author of the information. The declared relationship between the author and the original source adds credibility to the text being read, even if it is unknown to their audience.

2. The presence of trigger words in rumors and jokes that affect the human psyche and instincts. These words evoke emotions such as fear, excitement, curiosity, anger, sympathy in a person and move a person to action. Such words encourage the user to click the "like" or "send" button. Such words may include "false", "deceit", "exclusive", "true", "prohibited", "confidential" and other words with similar meanings.

3. Fakes are also spread by presenting the situation through a hero or an anti-hero. To the user, the event begins to remind them of certain individuals, which evoke feelings of sympathy or disgust, similar to trigger words.

4. Copying information when spreading fakes allows you to reach a wider audience. It will be possible to use Internet bots for this.

5. Visual lines are also very effective in spreading fakes. According to the authors of the aforementioned

---

Phys. Rev. E 76, 036117 – Published 27 September 2007 URL https://proxylibrary.hse.ru:2291/pre/abstract/10.1103/PhysRevE.76.036117

[55] Муратова Н. Fake news: медиада дезинформация [Матн]: қўлланма / Н. Муратова, Н. Тошпулатова, Г. Алимова. – Ташкент: "Innovatsion rivojlanish nashriyot-matbaa uyi", 2020. –Б.14.

article, fake information shared on social networks may lack one or more of the above criteria.

According to research by American scientists, a person needs to see / listen to an advertising message at least three times in order to pay attention to it. In particular, according to H. Kragman, "once is enough to perceive information, twice - to understand it, and three times - to form an attitude to the advertising message."[56].

The process described above is built as a "snowball effect": an idea is implanted in the human mind, which gradually grows larger with more and more new details, expert comments. Based on what a person has read, seen and heard, an opinion on a subject is formed, and it becomes difficult to change or reject itThe "snowball effect" is also relevant for the spread of fake news. Lisa Faccio and her colleagues conclude that when writing a rebuttal to a fake news story, it is necessary to repeat the name or details, only to replace the fake story with the original version in the minds of the readersFake news on social media spreads wider and faster than disavowing it. Researchers from the Massachusetts Institute of Technology studied the distribution of 126,000 real and fake news stories on Twitter from 2006 to 2017 and found that the most popular fake news reached 10,000 users. Only 1000 people saw the real news. Researchers attribute the popularity of fake news to the "newness" of the information they contain.

According to a study conducted by Jonas De Kersmaiker and Arne Rothes of the University of Gent, people with higher cognitive abilities were able to change their opinions about the story after reading a rebuttal to fake news, while people with lower cognitive abilities found it more difficult to change their first impressions. Here it is worth mentioning the phenomenon of post truth.

---

[56] Назайкин А.Н. Современное медиапланирование. Учебное пособие. Солон-пресс, 2016. ISBN: 978-5-91359-210-1. -С. 86.

According to the definition given in the Oxford dictionary, "post-truth is a situation in which objective facts are less important in shaping public opinion than appeals to emotions and personal beliefs". Fake news appeals directly to people's emotions, helping to shape public opinion, meaning the post creates the conditions for the truth to emerge. As mentioned earlier, it is more difficult for subscribers to reject fake messages than to trust them. In their research on fake news, American scientists have given a great place to social networks, especially Twitter and Facebook. They studied the relationship between a user's socioeconomic status and their exposure to false information. In particular, American scientists Andrew Hess, Jonathan Nagler and Joshua Tuck have proven that the activity of spreading fake news in social networks depends on the age of users. In their research, they proved that "fake news is often shared by Facebook users over 65 years old. Retirees were seven times more likely to share fake news on social media than 18- to 29-year-olds [57].

The unlimited possibilities of the modern Internet are seriously damaging the principle of truthfulness of information. According to researchers, Two factors are responsible for the wide spread of "fake news": 1) quantitative factor: the existence of a huge amount of information on the Internet, which cannot be checked; **2) quality factor is** a technological factor in which, due to new technologies, the means of collecting and storing information, as well as the entities that produce it and the channels of transmission, have increased. These are the reasons that lowered the status and position of traditional mass media. Due to the well-developed technical means of creating and spreading fake news in modern times,

---

[57] Тихонова М. Стратегия противодействия распространению ложных новостей в социальных сетях. ВКР. –Москва, 2019. – С. 21.//Word of the Year 2016 is... [Electronic resource]. URL: https://en.oxforddictionaries.com/word-of-the-year/word-of-the-year-2016.

malicious "storytellers" have always learned to use modern technology to create false material that matches and resembles reality. For example, on April 20, 2019, on the Facebook social network, "In the city of Namangan, employees of the Tax Inspection are checking the document of an entrepreneur in a neighboring cafe!" the content of the message was spread. The Press Service of the State Tax Committee of the Republic of Uzbekistan studied the circumstances mentioned in this report and expressed its reaction to it: *This situation was investigated by responsible specialists. On April 20, 2019, Namangan City State Tax Inspectorate "Additional Income Determination and Crime Prevention Department" by State Tax Senior Inspectors A.Samatov and N.Karimov, Namangan City, "Haqiqat" MFY, Boburshah Street, In accordance with the decision of the President of the Republic of Uzbekistan dated June 26, 2018 "On measures to radically improve the activities of the State Tax Service" in the shopping center owned by citizen H. Rahmonov, a taxpayer's passporting event was held. As it turned out, explanatory work was carried out in order to support honest entrepreneurs and provide assistance to ensure their transparencyPassporting is not a check! It is a preventive event in which the state tax service authorities draw up an inspection report, which serves as the basis for calculating taxes and other mandatory payments. In this case, it is not allowed to interfere in the financial and economic activities of the taxpayer, that is, to check.*

The indicated cases were not confirmed when studied by a special group. There was no disagreement between the employees of the state tax service and the businessman. It turned out that the post left on the author and the topic contained signs of defamation and defamation of DSXO employees. The State Tax Committee appreciates citizens' suggestions and opinions about the system and is always ready to cooperate with the public in ensuring the effectiveness of reforms in the field, but not only with slander! Let us remind you that providing false information and slander is a cause of liability in accordance with the established procedure, says the press service of the DSQ [58].

In the course of the globalization of information processes, the rise of such fakes has become a serious problem that depends on the professionalism of media workers on the one hand, and on the media literacy of information consumers on the other hand. The current development of the Internet and social media has created vast and unlimited conditions for each information consumer to fulfill the role of both an information distributor and a public journalist at the same time. Therefore, in recent years, non-professionals have had great opportunities to create "innovation". A person can spread a message of questionable origin to thousands of people with the movement of a single finger. In such circumstances, every citizen unknowingly becomes a link in the chain of deadly disinformation. An example of this is Yulia Antopropova's information about the flood that occurred in Crimea in 2012, about the opening of the Neberzhayev reservoir, which she published on "Live Journal", "Facebook", and "V Kontakte". This message caused a great uproar: "If it is not opened, it will block the water of Novorossiysk, if it is opened, Crimea will be washed away." Repetition of unconfirmed information created panic among people, and it took a lot of efforts by the government to stop it. The book "Fake News: Informational Mystification" by S. Raspopova, professor of the Higher School of Press and Media Industry of Moscow Polytechnic University, and E. Bogdan, Master of Applied Communications at Wageningen University and Research Center in the Netherlands, shows the mistakes made by journalists that cause fake news to appear. At the end of 2018, UNESCO published a guide for journalists called "Journalism, Fake News and Disinformation". It includes an analysis of best practices

---

[58] info@terabayt.uz. DIMAX. 22.04.2019.

around the world on the process of Fact-checking (fact-checking) in the world media, checking content on social networks, media literacy, combating online violence and other issues. In Russian scientific circles, the issue of the spread of false information in social networks has now begun to be studied. This was especially motivated by the need to identify fake news and disinformation spread during the Russian-Ukrainian war in 2022.

According to Pew Research, most Americans believe they can spot fakes. However, V. Rubin, an associate professor at the Laboratory of Language and Information Technology Research at Western University in Ontario, confidently admits that Internet users do not consciously check the authenticity of the information they receive. Many countries are trying to solve the problem of fake news by regulating it. For example, in the summer of 2018, Belarus adopted amendments to its media law, which allows the government to prosecute people who spread false information online[59].

Criminal responsibility for spreading fakes has been introduced in China. Social networks can only post news from officially registered media. Authors of microblogs should clarify and refute rumors. China also has a mobile app where citizens can complain about news stories that cause them to be insecure[60].

In Croatia, the government is developing a bill aimed at increasing media literacy. This law does not contain mandatory mechanisms to combat disinformation[61].

In India, the government periodically shuts down

---

[59] Ўша манба

[60] Тихонова М. Стратегия противодействия распространению ложных новостей в социальных сетях. ВКР. Москва 2019. //www.allbestru/.

[61] Ўша манба

the Internet to stop the spread of fake news. The country has a base of fake news spread on social media. In some states, citizens can be jailed for publishing false information that causes fear or anxiety in the community [62].

In Indonesia, the government blocks websites that publish content deemed harmful to society. The Indonesian government has a team that monitors social media traffic around the clock to detect misinformation online. The country has also launched a website where people can report suspected fake news and find out if it is true or not. Italy has created a portal where citizens can report disinformation. If the fact of the spread of false information is confirmed, then their author may be imprisoned [63].

In Kenya, people who knowingly share misleading information can be fined up to $50,000 or jailed for up to two years. In Malaysia, spreading fake news is punishable by up to six years in prison and a fine of US$128,000 [64].

In Singapore, the government has developed recommendations to introduce restrictions on combating disinformation at the legislative level and to increase the level of media literacy of the population.

South Korea is developing a law to limit the spread of fakes on the Internet. In the US, social networks must keep track of ad copy, publish it, and monitor who pays and how much they pay to prevent disinformation from advertising companies. Media literacy is taught in schools in some states, such as California.

A government group has been established in

---

[62] Ўша манба

[63] Ўша манба

[64] Тихонова М. Стратегия противодействия распространению ложных новостей в социальных сетях. ВКР. Москва 2019. //www.allbestru/.

Australia to identify and counter foreign disinformation campaigns. In Bangladesh, anyone who spreads false news against the government on social media can go to jail.

In Brazil, a special team was created to identify and reject fake news during the election period. Penalties for identified violations range from fines to eight years in prison. In addition, the Brazilian government signed an agreement with Facebook and Google, obligating these platforms to "combat disinformation created by third parties." France has strict restrictions on publishing content during election campaigns, particularly in the three months before any vote. The legislation gives authorities the power to remove fake content shared via social media and even block sites that publish it.

In March 2019, Russia introduced amendments to the Law "On Information, Information Technologies and Information Protection" and the Code of Administrative Offenses (KoAP), which provides for fines for spreading fake news. 30,000 to 100,000 rubles to citizens for disseminating fake information for the first time in these regulatory legal documents; from 60,000 to 200,000 rubles to officials; it is recognized that a fine from 200,000 to 500,000 rubles can be imposed on legal entities. Fines increase for repeated violations, as well as if false information interferes with the operation of critical facilities. Citizens from 100 thousand to 300 thousand rubles; officials - from 300 thousand to 600 thousand rubles; legal entities - will have to pay a fine from 500 thousand to 1 million rubles.

If the spread of fake news led to "death of a person, damage to human health or property, mass violation of public order and (or) public safety, stopping the operation of life-supporting facilities", fines for citizens - from 300 thousand to 400 thousand rubles; for officials - from 600 thousand to 900 thousand rubles; for legal entities - from 1 million to 1.5 million rubles/ In addition, a special section has been created on the website of the Ministry of Foreign Affairs of Russia, which rejects false information about the Russian Federation published in foreign media. In Kazakhstan, intentionally spreading false information is punishable by up to seven years in prison. Even in Uzbekistan, citizens who spread fake news can be prosecuted and imprisoned. "On amendments and additions to the Criminal and Criminal Procedure Codes of Uzbekistan and the Code of Administrative Responsibility of Uzbekistan" [65] According to the law, a fine of 11,150,000 soums is imposed for spreading rumors and fake information, belittling or discrediting a person in mass media, telecommunication networks or the Internet, and 22,300,000 soums for spreading information threatening public order or safety. If the spread of false information continues after the fine, the authority will be fined again. This time the fine is 89,200,000 soums. At the same time, it is reported that a repeated fine can be replaced by restriction of freedom for up to three years[66].

Thus, in many countries, the fight against fakes is understood not as a fight against all false information, but against information that insults the government and the existing structures. Legislation does not have clear criteria for determining the reliability of information, which means that any news not approved by the government can be recognized as fake. It should also be noted that in some countries, the fight against fake news is mentioned only during the pre-election period. The rest of the time, whistleblowers will not be prosecuted.

2.3. Technological factors in the spread of fake and disinformation

---

[65] https://sangzor.uz/ozi-nima-gap/

[66] Тихонова М. Стратегия противодействия распространению ложных новостей в социальных сетях. ВКР. Москва, 2019. – С.58. //www. allbestru/.

In a broad sense, researchers classify the concept of "Fake" into two, namely **material** and **immaterial**[67] categories. **Material** fakes include forgery of trademarks, technologies, medicines, works of art, etc. **Immaterial ones** include social networks (social networks, messengers), make-up, fake, false news, which is deliberately distributed using Internet resources and in some media. Also in social networks, fake accounts, edited photo and video images, and so on [68] can be included in immaterial fakes.

In accordance with the law of the Russian Federation on "informatisation, information technology and Information Protection" and amendments to **the code** of administrative offenses, "fake" is socially significant, but unreliable information (fake) distributed in the form of messages as reality through various communicational channels.[69] This kind of information could threaten the citizens' life and (or) health. Fake information may cause public disorder, baffle (or lead to stop fully) the process of residential objects, including transport, industry, energetical objects, social infrastructure, communicational objects and credit companies. Spreading this kind of information is restricted also through the internet.

"Informational wave" is a crucial notion in learning the technologies of spreading information. "Informational wave" – this is distribution of information. It happens when mass media gets in touch with its target

---

[67] Зырянова М.О. Способы противодействия распространению фейковой информации..// cyberleninka.ru.

[68] Зырянова М.О. Способы противодействия распространению фейковой информации..// cyberleninka.ru.

[69] Что такое фейковые новости и как за них будут наказывать? [Электронный ресурс] // Официальный сайт Государственной Думы РФ. URL: http://duma.gov.ru/news/29982/.

auditory. If there is no response reaction by the society, there will not be an informational wave.[70]

Russian researcher A. V. Bolotnov differentiates three types of information waves in his paper "Informationnie Volni i Type ix v sovremennom mediadikursei K postanovke problemi"[71]

1. According to the degree of impact on society, **strong and weak** waves are distinguished. Strong information waves lead to practical solutions.

2. Based on the duration of their presence in the Media space, however, it is also separated into **long and short** waves.

3. The third type of information Waves has the form of propagation in such a way as **cumulative resonance, cascade, funnel, prism,** and is distinguished from others in nature.

Cumulative resonance, according to the scientist, "deepens the knowledge of society about the info dodgery. An event or happening is lavishly enlarged with new details, which, in turn, increases the resonant response in the public".[72]

For example, in March 2007, the details of the Boing 2019 MAX crash in Ethiopia were accompanied by the CVs of victims, reviews of aviation industry experts, reviews of the Boing company, comparison with a similar Boing crash in Indonesia, the airline's refusal to drive the Boing 737 MAX, analytical materials on the safety of the 737 MAX model.

---

[70] Зырянова М.О. Способы противодействия распространению фейковой информации.//cyberleninka.ru. с 1-4

[71] Болотнов А.В. Информационные волны и их типы в современном медиадискурсе: к постановке проблемы. : к постановке проблемы // Вестник ТГПУ. 2015. №6 (159). URL:

[72] Болотнов А.В. Ўша манба

The information wave that propagates as a cascade also has a linear direction as well as slight connections by society. The event enters the information space, but quickly disappears. For example, it is reported in the Saratov media that on The Victory Day in may 2019, a poster with images of "Wermakht" soldiers was hung in the dormitory building of the "Vavilov" Agrarian University.

In the information Wave, which spreads in the "Voronka" (funnel) style, there is a return to the same information state in different contexts several times in different conditions. In this case, the infirmary opens up new interpretations. "Voronka" means the gradual development of the plot of the event, the increase in the relevant social activity associated with it, getting to the international level, the strengthening of all problem points and the emergence of a new conflict around the interests of the participants [73].

This can be cited as an example of domestic violence, which went as far as humiliating, offending, insulting and even killing one of the family members, and so on. Any news like that will force a repeated and repeated return to the federal law of February 2017 on the decriminalization of domestic violence. According to this, for the first time in a family when someone is bullied, even if serious physical damage was done, this is considered an administrative violation, not a criminal act. It is clear to all our citizens that the protection order against domestic violence in such cases has been put into practice in Uzbekistan. According to this, legal measures are taken against the bully person.

---

[73] Болотнов А.В. Информационные волны и их типы в современном медиадискурсе: к постановке проблемы // Вестник ТГПУ. 2015. №6 (159). URL: https://cyberleninka.ru/article/n/informatsionnye-volny-i-ih-tipy-v-sovremennom-mediadiskurse-k-postanovke-problemy.

Another type of Information wave is the prism. It is characterized by a subjective assessment of the event. This is typical for the owners of leading feedback, in particular for popular mass media presenters, personalities, such as TV presenter Ksenia Sobchak or video blogger Nikolai Sobolev. An example is the free look from video bloggers in the media of Uzbekistan.

Fake news is often delivered in a cumulative resonance or cascade fashion according to the form and nature of the transmission. "Social media highly contributes to the manipulation of fake news by various comments, such as: class (Odnoklassniki), reposts (Vkontakte), poems (Facebook), retweets (Twitter), likes (YouTube)"[74]. It should also be noted that the spread of fakes "is directly related to the use of manipulative (based on the intentions of the information source) or resonant (aimed at the reaction of the recipients) communication technologies, which are aimed at working with large groups of people, for example, representatives of an entire region"[75]. Both technologies are based on working with ideas and visions (social stereotypes) that exist in the public mind.

"**Manipulative technology** - this is a deliberate and conscious interaction of the receiving addressee to the addressee with the help of specially selected and pre-

---

[74] [74] Тихонова М. Стратегия противодействия распространению ложных новостей в социальных сетях. - ВКР по направлению 42.04.02 Журналистика студента группы МЖД 172 образовательной программы агистратуры «Журналистика данных».С. 23- 24.

[75] Гридчин А.А. Коммуникативные технологии регулирования региональных конфликтов // Вестник Волгоградского государственного университета. Серия7: Философия, социология и социальные технологии. Волгоград, 2009. № 1 (9). 105-109 бб.

prepared images"[76]. Thus, images of people, companies, objects and ideas based on public perceptions (social stereotypes) can be used. At the same time, such visions can differ depending on the geographic, social, gender identity of the addressee. Such images always work in accordance with the purpose set by this source of communication. The image is created by" strengthening and exaggerating some characteristics of the object, minimizing or eliminating others, depending on the task that the speaker solves. As a result, the recipient will experience informational-psychological effects and will be confused"[77]. (In the case of manipulative methods and technologies, let's dwell more broadly in the first paragraph of the third chapter).

Resonant technologies are based not on the "introduction of new information, but on the adherence to ideas (social stereotypes) that exist in the public consciousness and the acquisition of feedback from the public in the form of an expected action"[78]. This aspect is based on the spread of anecdotes and rumors. It is the use of resonant technologies that leads to the popularization of fakes at tremendous speeds, thereby disrupting stability in society and the onset of panic. The resonant effect model would "reinforce stereotypes already present in the minds of the masses; convert them into verbal and visual form and (or) event form (people believe what they see with

---

[76] Зырянова М.О. Способы противодействия распространению фейковой информации.//cyberleninka.ru С.1-4.

[77] Makovich G.V. Communicative technologies in professional group activities [Электронный ресурс] // Management Issues. 2019. № 03 (58). URL: http://vestnik.uapa.ru/en/issue/2014/03/21. Зырянова М.О. Способы противодействия распространению фейковой информации.// cyberleninka.ru. – С. 1-4

[78] Зырянова М.О. Способы противодействия распространению фейковой информации//cyberleninka.ru.С.1-4.

their own eyes); rely on structural components such as reinforcing the message with signs of truthfulness"[79].

On February 1 in 2020, a media report appeared about a criminal case filed against a Latvian citizen in order to spread false evidence about the coronavirus[80]. According to the Latvian media, a person posts a video on social networks about the fact that the first coronavirus disease was recorded in Latvia. But in early February 2020, New coronavirus cases in Latvia were not officially confirmed. Minister of health of Latvia I. Vinkele In an interview with "Baltkom" radio, he claimed that he was worried about the panic on social media, not the spread of the virus itself[81].

In general, at the beginning of February 2020, international organizations recorded more than 200 fakes about the coronavirus. This is stated by the official representative of the Ministry of health of the Republic of Kazakhstan D. Akhmetsharip reported in a briefing[82].

---

[79] Почепцов Г.Г. Информационные войны. М., 2001. –С.138.

[80] В Латвии возбудили дело за распространение фейков о коронавирусе [Электронный ресурс] // РИА «Новости». URL: https://ria.ru/20200201/1564132102.html (дата обращения: 25.02.2020)

[81] Винькеле: Латвия полностью готова к встрече с коронавирусом [Электронный ресурс] // Новостное агентство "Sputnik". URL: https://lv.sputniknews.ru/Latvia/20200210/13195694/Vinkele-Latviya-polnostyu-gotova-k-vstreche-s-koronavirusom.html (дата обращения: 25.02.2020)

[82] Тулеубекова А. Н.-С. Почти 200 фейков о коронавирусе зафиксировали Международные организации [Электронный ресурс] // Сетевое издание "Zakon.kz". URL: https://www.zakon.kz/5005826-pochti-200-feykov-o-koronaviruse.html (дата обращения: 20.06.2020)

According to him, some users of social networks in Canada, Latvia, Hong Kong, Thailand, Malaysia, Indonesia and China were arrested for spreading fake information about the coronavirus[83].

In early February 2020, the Director General of the World Health Organization (WHO), T. Gebreyesus appealed to the world community to stand against the spread of fakes associated with the spread of coronavirus. He noted that the WHO not only fights the virus, but also resists the spread of fakes about this disease[84].

In the context of digitization of society and the widespread use of digital technologies, the need to ensure the comprehensive safety of young people and adults, the issues of fighting with the spread of fake data are of great importance. In addition, administratively this issue has already been resolved through the introduction of relevant laws and the work of law enforcement agencies. However, this work should also be done in the PR field.

It should be noted that rumors, suspicions, false information appear when a shortage of true facts occurs in the information space. Most often, fakes arise, first of all, against the background of situations associated with a threat to life, well-being or serfdom. The spread of rumors is caused by factors such as "the importance of the issues

---

[83] Тулеубекова А. Н.-С. Ряд пользователей соцсетей арестованы за распространение фэйков про коронавирус [Электронный ресурс] // Там же. URL: https://www.zakon.kz/5006009-ryad-polzovateley-sotssetey-arestovany.html (дата обращения: 29.02.2020)

[84] Глава ВОЗ призвал бороться с дезинформацией в связи со вспышкой коронавируса [Электронный ресурс] // Информационное агентство «ТАСС». URL: https

under consideration, the presence of serious organizational problems"[85].

Before starting the fight against fakes, it is necessary to analyze the cause, sources of rumors and the degree of their spread. It is necessary to promptly provide complete and reliable information about the problem to both the media and social networks and messengers, which are the main sources of fakes. It is also necessary to support people who can influence the formation of public opinion. It should be noted that the principles of fighting against the spread of unreliable information through the media, social networks and messengers are very similar.

The easiest way to reduce the amount of distributed fake data is to fill the information space with reliable official data. This can be done by sending official press releases through traditional media, organizing interviews with speakers, press conferences, and other press events. It is also necessary to carry out this work on social networks and messengers.

The work can also be done through official accounts, large informal groups that are popular among users. In addition, using targeted (target) advertising can also be effective. The main thing is that this work is carried out in regular order and the information space is filled with the correct information about what is happening.

Another way to fight against the spread of Fake data is to ignore it, if it is purposeful and this information does not harm anyone, namely, to silence the reaction to it. Usually, if fake information is not "fed up" with new messages, any discussions will stop on their own as early as a week.

If fakes are distributed, then it is necessary to deal with their rejection by distributing detailed reliable

---

[85] Королько В.Г. Основы паблик релейшнз. М., 2000. 343 б.
Зырянова М.О. Способы противодействия распространению фейковой информации.// cyberleninka.ru. С 1-4.

information. This work should be started from the sites where the spread of those fakes began.

Digitalization, which peaked at the beginning of the 21st century, spurred the development of global diversity in the media. The digitization process has shifted almost all media and technical devices to digital. As a result, the number of radio stations and TV channels increased, individual services of cellular communication and multipurpose devices intended for transmitting and receiving signals began to become popular. Digital technologies have contributed to the loss of the boundary between different media appearances. One online service includes news, video, music, messaging and other services. In the era of digital communication, the ability to create a media product by users expanded and gained a variety of content. Moving from a traditional communication model based on the "one with many" principle, typical of Radio, television and print media, to a "majority with many "model that applies the" collaborative creation and use" is considered as the most important part of digital media development[86].

Information society is such a society in which all relations and connections between people are built on the basis of information exchange. Information in such a society serves as an inexhaustible main source of raw materials for all.

Thanks to information, the education system will be rebuilt in a new society, a new limit of scientific research will be established, mass communications will reorganize itself. The information society is the result of the rapid development of electronic computing techniques and Audiovisual Media. In this, the post-industrial society becomes a Textron society, and on its basis a globalized communication system is formed. In its Medium, people accept the global appearance of the universe, relying on

---

[86] Зырянова М.О. Способы противодействия распространению фейковой информации.//cyberleninka.ru.C1-4.

symbols and feelings. The new generation will not be obsessed with reading literature based on ideological-structural analysis or a detailed statement to understand the universe, but it will feel and understand the universe through the means of audiovisual communications. It is theoretically justified that the Textron information society is not of ideological or social content. It is of a spatial and temporal nature, embracing the entire universe with new and modern means of Audiovisual Communication. For example, in 2014, journalist Craig Silverman and the Center for Digital Journalism at Columbia University provided an Emergent service that automatically refutes rumors and lies published on the Internet [87]. The site concentrates media materials, collects on the topic. The system determines the original source by the number of links assigned to it. Every hour, the algorithm of this site monitors the changes in them, if changes are made to the headers. Determines the validity coefficient of information based on the data collected.

As of 2015, Facebook has provided users with the ability to complain about it if the messages on the tape contain false information. To do this, it is necessary to select "Leave a comment about this publication" mark "FAKE NEWS" and send a comment. The news, which causes doubts from users, is checked by a group of journalists, if the news turns out to be a Fake, then this content is deleted.

In 2016, Facebook began to reduce its coverage of posts with sensational headlines in an effort to convince maximum users to go to the page where the material was given and to convey their content in the best possible way. "The title often includes trigger-words and capitalized

---

[87] Тихонова М. Стратегия противодействия распространению ложных новостей в социальных сетях. ВКР. М. 2019. – С. 24 //www. allbestru/.

words that evoke different emotions in the reader, such as fear"[88].

In April 2019, Facebook announced that it had entered into a partnership agreement with The Associated Press to investigate the news. By doing so, it was stated that the coverage of disinformation publishing groups would be reduced, with low-quality publications on the tape having appropriate labels. A confidence indicator will also appear in English and Spanish[89]. Facebook also began blocking accounts of users who spread fake news and used fake news.

However, Facebook algorithms are not always able to correctly identify fakes in Russian. In April 2019, an advertisement was distributed on Facebook saying "make a survey in 5 minutes and get from 125,000 rubles". It was accompanied by the Sberbank logo and photos of famous media. But this fake was not blocked by Facebook.

Twitter, in turn, prohibits the creation of multiple accounts that share the same information. With this, the distribution of Fake data using bots on the network was prevented.

Russia does not have a complex approach to identifying and rejecting fake news. Nevertheless, the rejection of fakes is becoming a hobby of the journalistic community. For example, the Russian social network "Vkontakte", following the example of Facebook, made it possible for users to complain about distracting content.

Conclusions on chapter II

Thus, fake data is, first of all, a means of influencing a certain audience, which is very common in the Internet environment due to its convenience, scale and

---

[88] Ўша ерда

[89] Remove, Reduce, Inform: New Steps to Manage Problematic Content. [Электронный ресурс: https://newsroom.fb.com/news/2019/04/remove-reduce-inform-new-steps/]

high speed of information dissemination. The variety of implementation of this linguistic phenomenon even in a nonlinear way allows its types to be classified in detail according to various criteria (time of appearance, topic of speech, field of activity, form of existence, level of described events, purpose of the message). By Custom, each feature in them is closely related to another, which determines the coexistence of fakes.

The prevalence of fakes and disinformations is similar in terms of characteristics. They are delivered to the general public using both non electronic and electronic media. So if there is a desired audience, distribution tools and methods for their distribution, that is all enough.

Because of the huge threat of fake linguistic and nonlinguistic information to society and people's lives, fighting against it internationally has become an urgent global problem. The era itself demands that in this struggle not only the creators of information, but also the consumers of information become active. In this sense, it is important to promote media and information literacy among users of information and teach it.

CHAPTER III.
MEDIA KNOWLEDGE AS A FACTOR OF FIGHTING AGAINST INFORMATINOAL ATTACKS
3.1. Technologies for spreading extremist content on social networks

As everything that created by humanity has both positive and negative affects, unfortunately, the Internet Network, the Cyberspace is doomed to serve both good and evil at the same time. It is known that the internet has long been used not only by humanitarian people engaged in some profitable business or some other activity, but also by terrorists and extremists in their desire to achieve their own mercenary intentions by intimidating, manipulating people who are facing them.

The high level of anonymity on the internet and the extreme democratization of communication have had exactly the same negative consequences as described above. In recent years, extremist ideas have become significantly active in cyberspace. The mechanism that prevents the mass manifestation of extremism on the pages of national newspapers and TV channels does not work on the Internet. This creates a favorable environment for the promotion of extremist ideas. This made it possible to have all access to information of extremist content. Sites of similar information on the internet can be easily found by any reader or student. That is why the Internet global network is being evaluated by extremist ideologists as a very favorable platform for ideological propaganda and struggle.

It is important to understand the role of the Internet in the development of extremism and to understand the relevant terms in order not to fall into the internet trap of extremists, as well as to study the legal assessment of the phenomenon of extremism.

<u>Extremism</u> (France. extremism, ot lat. extremus-extreme)-compliance with extreme opinions and measures (S. I. Ojegov, N. Yu. Shvedova Explanatory Dictionary of the Russian language. – M., 2000).

"Paragraph 1 of Article 3 (1) of the" Shanghai convention on terrorism, separatism and the fight against extremism" [90] defines the concept of "extremism" as follows: extremism means any action aimed at forcibly occupying power or forcibly holding power, as well as forcibly changing the state's constitutional system, as well as violent encroachment on public security, including the establishment of illegal armed structures or participation in them. Terrorism is an extreme manifestation of

---

[90] Шанхайская конвенция о борьбе с терроризмом, сепаратизмом и экстремизмом. Шанхай, 15 июня 2001 г. Ратифицирована Постановлением ОМРУз от 30 августа 2001 года N 274-II https://nrm.uz/contentf?doc=51369

extremism. Many examples of this can be found in the internet space.

After a series of terrorist attacks, the topic of fighting against extremism rose sharply again. Researchers[91] give a number of examples. For example, on October 31, 2015, a Russian plane crashed in the Sinai Peninsula (Egypt), 224 people died. The cause of the crash is a terrorist attack. In Beirut, Lebanon, another powerful explosion thundered in the same crowd. 44 people died. The situation in Paris caused the greatest resonance among the world community. On the evening of November 13, explosions rumbled near the Stade De France, terrorists also captured hostages and opened fire on the "Bataclan" club, while warriors also shot at the restaurant's open porch. Approximately 130 people were placed on the casualty list, with over 350 injured. Most of the terrorists suspected of involvement in the incident were arrested or destroyed.

Extremism, according to custom, is based on a certain ideology. Signs of extremism include ideologies based on affirming that an individual has uniqueness, superiority or disadvantage based on social, racial, national, religious or linguistic affiliation or attitude to religion, as well as political, ideological, racial, national ideas, and express religious hatred or hostility against any social group. Followers of such ideology engage in extremist activities. In particular, they distribute extremist material on the internet, whether they realize it or not, they violate a law and it is inevitable that they will be prosecuted.

Mainly, following types of extremist data can be found on the internet more often:

---

[91] Экстремизм в сети Интернет: как не попасть в ловушку. // https://ntstiso.ru/wp-content/uploads/2021/05/ Ищенкова М. С. Проблемы привлечения к уголовной ответственности при осуществлении экстремистской деятельности в сети Интернет. // http://www.ling-expert.ru/conference/

1. Programmatic documents of various groups containing information that promotes the violent transformation of the constitutional order and the violation of the integrity of the country.

2. In the internet space, it is often possible to face the propaganda of the uniqueness, superiority of citizens in terms of social, racial, national, religious or language. Since there is no censorship on the internet, it is a democratic space. Therefore, in this space, the spread of any, including extremist ideology, around the world becomes easier.

3. Today, symbols of Nazism are often displayed on social networks, and Nazi ideas are promoted. For example, with the inclusion of the Nazi word in the search, one can see the names of a huge number of groups. But it is illegal to distribute such and similar information on the Internet.

As an example, it can cited the fact that the United States has also been conducting research on the online activities of the terrorist organization Al-Qaeda for a long time (Al-Qaeda is considered one of the first extremist organizations that began to actively use the internet in their activities).

Al-Qaeda activists have become proficient, a master of internet propaganda, recruitment, fundraising for the purchase of new weapons. One of the articles on Terrorism published in the United States quoted: "If the FBI(FBR)has something that hates O'sama bin Laden even more, it is O'sama bin Laden's use of the internet"[92]. Islamic extremists have also produced specially trained people, namely "media jihad fighters", who sit on Facebook and other social networks and participate in

---

[92] Экстремизм в сети Интернет: как не попасть в ловушку // https://ntstiso.ru/wp-content/. Ушенина А.С. Проблемы привлечения к уголовной ответственности при осуществлении экстремистской деятельности в сети Интернет (статья) Уральская Государственная Юридическая Академия, Екатеринбург. – 2009.

neutral discussions, significantly promoting their views. Through their efforts, Al-Qaeda and other similar organization ranks were noted to be filled by several hundred warriors each year.

To be able to resist extremist propaganda, it is important to know the methods that extremists actively use. These methods are largely based on lies, i.e. Fake.

One of the most commonly used methods is the deliberate false interpretation of history. This method is aimed at gradually changing the social worldview in a person. The myth of the centuries-old and relentless war of the peoples of the Caucasus with Russia is spreading. Relatively recent history facts are also being distorted. For example, an article posted on the "Ichkeria" website falsely stated: "until the advent of the new Moscow (before the adoption of the 1993 Constitution), 12 sovereign states, including the Chechen Republic, had been formed". A game of such dates and a violation of the chronology of events allows separatists to characterize the actions of the federal forces as "invasion".

Another popular method is <u>to create a presence effect</u>. This is achieved by posting videos allegedly taken from the "Military-Combat Action site" on websites. On some sites, the warriors also posted video appeals with threats against the "invaders" and "national traitors", calling on young people for armed actions and acts of terrorism.

In addition, the method of exaggerating the negative characteristics and failures of the opponent is also often used. Representations of Russia in deliberately unpleasant images are also used. Some Internet sites also feature headlines such as "Russia's economy is on the brink of collapse", " Russia is a fake Great State", "a quarter of Russia's population is mentally ill". Such a method is now often used in the process of creating information flows regarding the war between Russia and Ukraine.

Another very common method of extremist Internet resources is factographic propaganda, in which" in fact politically oriented information is presented under the guise of unbiased news"[93]. For example, extremists doubt the accuracy of information coming from Russian sources. Knowing history well, being able to expose the false rhetoric of extremists is one of the very effective ways to combat the propaganda of extremism on the global network.

Uzbekistan also has significant results in combating terrorist and extremist content. As a result of the work carried out in the direction of information security in 2016-2017 alone, 100,000 internet resources, consisting of more than 4 million information materials of a terrorist and extremist nature, were deleted from the network or blocked from its activities"[94].

In social networks, young people spend more of their time than in the older generation. According to the researchers' observation, currently 90% of young people turn to the Internet as the main source of information. Modern youth can now be observed using mainly social networks and video - and audioportals such as "Twitter", "Facebook", "Odnoklassniki", "YouTube" on a large scale[95]. Older people do not have or do not have enough time for such work and do not even have the habit of spending their free time in this way. Young people who are passionate about the possibility of self-expression on

---

[93] Экстремизм в сети Интернет: как не попасть в ловушку // https://ntstiso.ru/wp-content/

[94] Машарипов Б. Ўзбекистоннинг терроризм ва экстремизмга қарши кураш хамда жаҳонда тинчлик ва
барқарорликни таъминлашдаги роли. // https://stopterror.uz/uz/ 12.07.2019.

[95] Маматкулов А.А. Ўқувчи- ёшлар ўртасида интернет ва ижтимоий тармоқлардан фойдаланиш маданиятини шакллантириш.// Замонавий таълим / Современное образование 2020, 6 (91).-Б.17-23.

the internet are actively involved in virtual communication. If they do not have enough media literacy and media immune, they will easily become the prey of virtual extremists.

Studies have shown that youth make up the majority of extremist groups. Individuals between the ages of 14 and 22 are the most dangerous for mastering extremist ideas. Those of this age are characterized by a strong sense of justice, the meaning of life and the focus on the search for values.

According to international experts, about 300,000 representatives of the younger generation who have not reached the age of 18 are among a number of religious-extremist groups around the world. In particular, according to the Brooklyn Institute, the number of accounts linked to the Islamic State terrorist group to one degree or another on the Twitter network reaches 90,000, and each has more than 1,000 students. The bulk of the visitors are teenagers and girls"[96].

President of Russia V. Putin said at the 4th of March in 2015. meeting of the expanded collegium of the country's HIV, "extremists poison society with the poison of warrior nationalism, intolerance and aggression. We know very well what this can lead to, following the example of a neighboring country — Ukraine." That is why the problem of fighting against extremist ideology still does not lose its relevance, and even then.[97]

Unfortunately, there are fewer threats and to reduce such violations, it is mandatory that everyone who uses information and media has access to media knowledge, media immunity.

---

[96] // https://stopterror.uz/uz/ Машарипов Б. Ўзбекистоннинг терроризм ва экстремизмга қарши кураш хамда жаҳонда тинчлик ва барқарорликни таъминлашдаги роли. 12.07.2019

[97] Ўша ерда

The fight against terrorism-related crimes, which is extremism and its most terrible manifestation, "is considered one of the actual problems that worries the world community today. These crimes are not limited to the territory of one state, but are gaining a transnational scale".[98]

Uzbekistan, like other countries that respect its independence and sovereignty, has been a constant participant and initiator of this process, considering the fight against extremism and terrorism as an important factor in ensuring global security.

"In the first years of independence, Uzbekistan felt extremist and terrorist threats in its "body"[99]. At that time, a group of extremists demanded to change the political system in the country, establish an Islamic caliphate, and rule the country based on Sharia norms. Based on this plan, the extremists sought to seize power by force. In order to threaten stability and peace in our multi-ethnic society, religious extremist and international terrorist organizations tried to form groups fighting for power by means of militancy, encourage and support them in every way. The danger of religious extremism and international terrorism for Central Asian countries in Namangan and Andijan in 1990, during the civil war in Tajikistan in 1990-1996, in Tashkent on February 16, 1999, in Batken of Kyrgyzstan, Surkhandarya and Tashkent regions of Uzbekistan in 1999-2001, In March-April 2004, in Tashkent city and Bukhara region, in July 2004 in Tashkent city, in May

---

[98] // https://stopterror.uz/uz/ Машарипов Б. Ўзбекистоннинг терроризм ва экстремизмга қарши кураш хамда жаҳонда тинчлик ва барқарорликни таъминлашдаги роли. 12.07.2019

[99] [99] // https://nuz.uz/uz/zhamoat/Аҳмедов Т. Ўзбекистонда экстремизмга қарши кураш борасидаги ёндашувлар концептуал жиҳатдан ўзгармоқда- 06.04.2021// https://nuz.uz/uz/zhamoat/

2005 in Andijan in May 2005, it manifested itself clearly[100].

Even in the conditions of increasing terrorist attacks and increasing direct threats to the country's stable development, the government of the Republic of Uzbekistan managed to neutralize radical groups and take strict legal measures against the participants of terrorist activities. Such activities were aimed at ensuring the safety of the population of our country and creating stable socio-political conditions in the country.

As of today, "Based on the decision of the Supreme Court of December 24, 2021, 19 channels (groups, material) on social networks were found to be extremist and terrorist and are prohibited to import, distribute, prepare or show on the territory of Uzbekistan".[101] 8 of them operate on Telegram messenger, 8 more on Facebook and 3 on Instagram platforms.

In the general list provided by the Ministry of Justice, the number of pages and channels deemed extremist and terrorist is about 150. These web pages violate "Article 11 of the Counter-Extremism Act".

According to it, if the materials imported, prepared, stored, distributed and displayed on mass media in the territory of Uzbekistan openly encourage the implementation of extremist activities, they will be considered extremist materials by the court, and their import, preparation, storage, distribution and

---

[100] //https://savollar.muslimaat.uz//Ёқубова О. Ўзбекистоннинг диний экстремизм ва халқаро терроризмга қарши глобал курашдаги ўрни

[101] //https://savollar.muslimaat.uz/Ёқубова О. Ўзбекистоннинг диний экстремизм ва халқаро терроризмга қарши глобал курашдаги ўрни //https://savollar.muslimaat.uz/

demonstrations are prohibited according to the law"[102]. In the current era, extremism and terrorism have become a complex socio-political phenomenon that has gained an international scale and embodies problems of a political, economic, territorial, spiritual, moral and religious nature. Today, religious extremism and international terrorism threaten not only the external but also the internal security of the countries of the world. "Nowadays, the processes of violent extremism and radicalization leading to terrorism are increasing globally. It is absolutely "dangerous" to not take proactive measures against these processes and to assume that this problem is solely the responsibility of each country's law enforcement agencies and security services"[103].

Speaking about the concept of "violent extremism and radicalism" (VERLT) leading to terrorism, it should also be mentioned that many countries have adopted their own definitions of terrorism and violent extremism. In the Republic of Uzbekistan, the concept of "violent extremism" is not used, but only the concept of "extremism" is used.[104]

Eliminating extremism in modern conditions requires not ending the activity of a certain group or bringing their "leaders" to justice, but fighting against its very ideology, eliminating its causes and factors. In the work of the First President of the Republic of Uzbekistan,

---

[102] /https://www.gazeta.uz/uz/2022/01/25. Ижтимоий тармоқлардаги экстремистик ва террористик деб топилган саҳифалар рўйхати янгиланди. // Янгиликларимиз халқ учун.

[103] /https://savollar.muslimaat.uz/ Ёкубова О. Ўзбекистоннинг диний экстремизм ва халқаро терроризмга қарши глобал курашдаги ўрни //https://savollar.muslimaat.uz/

[104] Маматова Я.М., Арифханова С.Н. Зўравон экстремизмнинг олдини олиш: масс-медиада ёритиш масалалари. Ўқув қўлланма – Т.: VNESHINVESTPROM 2020. – Б. 12.

I. A. Karimov, "High Spirituality - Invincible Power", based on the idea of "Enlightenment against ignorance", the task of preventing the spread of the "virus" of violent ideology, the formation of religious and moral consciousness in young people and their ideological upbringing based on enlightenment, was defined as the main link.

If the spread of extremist ideas and ideology, especially through the Internet is not prevented, the number of such militant groups will continue to increase. "Despite the fact that not a single terrorist act has been committed in Uzbekistan in the last ten years, an example of this is the participation of the country's citizens in hostilities in Syria, Iraq and Afghanistan. At the same time, the terrorist acts committed by persons of Uzbek origin in the USA, Sweden and Turkey also showed the need to reconsider the approach to the solution of this problem, to fight against religious fanaticism among the population, and to pay great attention to increasing the effectiveness of preventive measures".[105]

Taking into account all the dangers and threats of the era of globalization today, on the ratification of the Convention against Terrorism of the Shanghai Cooperation Organization (Yekaterinburg, June 16, 2009) in Uzbekistan, on the Eurasian Group to Combat Money Laundering and Terrorist Financing On ratification of the Agreement (Moscow, June 16, 2011), "On Combating Money Laundering, Financing of Terrorism, and Financing of Proliferation of Weapons of Mass Destruction", "On Combating Terrorism", "Combating Extremism" laws "On the State Security Service of the Republic of Uzbekistan", resolutions of the Prime Ministry and the Cabinet of Ministers, Resolutions and Decrees of the President of the Republic of Uzbekistan

---

[105] // https://stopterror.uz/uz/ Машарипов Б. Ўзбекистоннинг терроризм ва экстремизмга қарши кураш хамда жаҳонда тинчлик ва барқарорликни таъминлашдаги роли. 12.07.2019.

were adopted. "The adoption of these regulatory legal documents serves to ensure the constitutional rights and freedoms of the country's citizens, as well as the guarantees of a peaceful and prosperous life. Our republic has ratified many (total 12[106]) international treaties aimed at combating terrorism and consistently fulfills its obligations".[107]

According to the Law "On Combating Extremism"[108] in Uzbekistan on July 30, 2018, Uzbek and foreign citizens, as well as stateless persons, who engaged in extremist activities, are liable according to the law.

The law states that a person will be released from responsibility in accordance with the law if he voluntarily refuses to participate in extremist activities, informs the relevant state authorities about it, and actively helps to prevent the occurrence of serious consequences and the realization of the goals of extremists.[109]

On September 19, 2018, another Presidential Decree "On improving the procedure for acquitting citizens of the Republic of Uzbekistan who have mistakenly joined terrorist, extremist or other prohibited

---

[106] https://savollar.muslimaat.uz/. Ёкубова О. Ўзбекистоннинг диний экстремизм ва халқаро терроризмга қарши глобал курашдаги ўрни //

[107] https://nuz.uz/uz/zhamoat/// Темур Аҳмедов. Ўзбекистонда экстремизмга қарши кураш борасидаги ёндашувлар концептуал жиҳатдан ўзгармоқда- 06.04.2021// https://nuz.uz/uz/zhamoat/

[108] qarash.uz.// Ўзбекистон Республикасининг "Экстремизмга қарши курашиш тўғрисида"ги қонуни.

[109] https://aniq.uz/yangiliklar «Террористик, экстремистик ёки бошқа тақиқланган ташкилот ва гуруҳлар таркибига адашиб кириб қолган Ўзбекистон Республикаси фуқароларини жиноий жавобгарликдан озод этиш тартибини такомиллаштириш тўғрисида» 2018 йил 19 сентябр ПФ.

organizations and groups from criminal responsibility" was announced. This decree allowed the citizens who were mistakenly included in the extremist groups, who were outside the territory of our country, who realized the illegality of their actions and went on the path to recovery, to return to their homeland, to their families, to a peaceful life. In the first year, the commission created in accordance with the decree considered the appeals submitted for release from criminal liability of 40 citizens who mistakenly joined the prohibited organizations. The main goal was to create conditions for such people to feel themselves under the protection and care of the state, as full-fledged citizens. Using the method of bringing administrative and criminal responsibility to citizens who are already not very dangerous for the state and society can cause them to become more angry and act against the state.

In recent years, the scope of work aimed at directing the policy of humanity and forgiveness characteristic of our people against extremist ideas has been expanded. In particular, more than 20,000 citizens considered to be connected to extremist groups in our country were removed from a special account and the practice of keeping such lists was completely abandoned. From 2017 to today, more than 4,000 people convicted of extremism have been legally forgiven.[110]

Until now, the Republic of Uzbekistan has accepted extremism within the framework of organizations such as the UN, the Organization for Security and Cooperation in Europe (OSCE), the Commonwealth of Independent States (CIS), the Shanghai Cooperation Organization (SCO), the Eurasian Economic Cooperation Organization (EOEC), the Organization of the Islamic Conference (OIC) and has been actively

---

[110] https://nuz.uz/uz/zhamoat/Темур Ахмедов. Ўзбекистонда экстремизмга қарши кураш борасидаги ёндашувлар концептуал жиҳатдан ўзгармоқда- 06.04.2021

participating in the implementation of documents and agreements related to the fight against international terrorism.

Today, the joint fight against terrorism, extremism, and the spread of narcotics, along with cooperation in the political, economic, cultural and humanitarian spheres, among the SCO member states, is an important factor in strengthening regional security and stability.

The activeness of Uzbekistan in the fight against terrorism and extremism can be explained by the fact that it regularly participates in the work of the CIS Anti-Terror Center and that the center is located in the city of Tashkent.

Currently, special importance is being paid to raising legal culture, religious and moral enlightenment among the population of the country, mainly among the youth.

Systematic work is being carried out on social rehabilitation, bringing back to normal life those who have been influenced by extremist ideas and have realized their mistake.

Great attention is being paid to forming an attitude of intolerance towards extremism in society, eliminating the causes, factors and conditions that cause extremism. Complex measures, including ideological and practical efforts, are being implemented in this regard. The Committee on Religious Affairs, the Ministry of Internal Affairs, the Ministry of Neighborhood and Family Support, and the Youth Union of Uzbekistan are also involved in ideological work.

Within the framework of the new system developed in the fight against extremism: 1) explaining the main goals, tasks and principles of state policy in the field of religion to the general public, leaders and employees of state and public organizations, increasing their activity and initiative; 2) development of religious and secular views of the population and, especially, the young generation; 3) it is determined to ensure wide promotion of our national traditions and values against radical ideas spread in mass media, internet sites and social networks.[111] The main reason for this is that there are cases of giving a religious tone to the socio-political processes taking place in our country, interpreting false ideas as original religious values, and inculcating unhealthy beliefs among the population.

In the practical direction, citizens who have repented of their actions and returned to a peaceful way of life, as well as persons who are inclined to participate in the activities of extremist or other prohibited organizations and groups, are provided with employment, social support, and help in establishing business activities.

Special attention was also paid to working with the representatives of the category most affected by extremist ideas, that is, women and young people. The main goal is to provide both ideological and practical support to such individuals who are prone to fall under the influence of extremist ideas, as well as to reduce the social base of extremists.

Today, religious extremism and international terrorism have become not only external, but also internal security issues for the countries of the world, so preventive measures against extremist ideas are being actively implemented not only inside the country, but also abroad. A clear example of this is the "Mehr" humanitarian operation, which began in 2019 and aims to evacuate citizens of Uzbekistan from the Middle East and Afghanistan. In particular, during 2019-2020, 318 citizens of Uzbekistan, mostly women and children, were returned to their homeland.[112] Before returning these persons to

---

[111] https://nuz.uz/uz/zhamoat/ Темур Аҳмедов. Ўзбекистонда экстремизмга қарши кураш борасидаги ёндашувлар концептуал жиҳатдан ўзгармоқда- 06.04.2021

[112] // https://stopterror.uz/uz/ Машарипов Б. Ўзбекистоннинг терроризм ва экстремизмга қарши кураш хамда жаҳонда тинчлик ва барқарорликни таъминлашдаги роли. 12.07.2019.

Uzbekistan, interviews were held with them, and citizens who regret their actions and intend to return to a peaceful way of life were selected. Currently, regular individual and targeted work is being carried out for the rehabilitation of repatriated persons and their social adaptation to society.

Attention is also paid to migrant workers, who are more likely to fall into the hands of extremists. Groups consisting of representatives of the Ministry of Internal Affairs, the Committee on Religious Affairs, the Office of Muslims of Uzbekistan, the Youth Union and other public organizations regularly conduct preventive measures among Uzbek labor migrants and students in Russia and Kazakhstan. In it, special emphasis is placed on conversations about not falling under the influence of extremist ideas, providing legal and social assistance to citizens in difficult social situations. A clear example of this is the activity of the Internet radio channel "Voice of the Fatherland". Stopterror.uz site contains materials of this radio.

The change of views on the fight against extremism is highly appreciated by the world community. On the one hand, this is having its effect from the point of view of security, and on the other hand, as a result of the reforms, citizens' confidence in the government has increased, and it has led to the formation of a new model of relations between the state and the population, based on the creation of conditions for the guarantees of religious freedom of the population. The basis of this model is the strengthening of the traditions of Islamic enlightenment and religious tolerance. Such an approach will undoubtedly bear fruit in the near future.[113]

In general, to prevent the growing young generation from falling under the influence of terrorism

---

[113] // https://nuz.uz/uz/zhamoat/Аҳмедов. Ўзбекистонда экстремизмга қарши кураш борасидаги ёндашувлар концептуал жиҳатдан ўзгармоқда. - 06.04.2021// https://nuz.uz/uz/zhamoat/

and extremism, to protect young people from various ideological and informational attacks propagated through the Internet, to further expand the scope of activities for the formation of youth with broad knowledge and high thinking, against the ideas of terrorism and extremism It is appropriate to prepare and publish comprehensive scientific researches and books, promote the idea of tolerance and the idea of strengthening peace, organize seminars and conferences on the true essence of Islam, and further increase the role of civil society institutions in this direction.

Manipulative technologies of fakes on social media:

Today, the development of science and technology occurs due to the unlimited possibilities of the Internet, which has led to the improvement of interstate communication tools. Also, the opportunities offered by this network serve to satisfy the information needs in several areas of human life. As technology advances and users are now proud of their phones as smart assistants, the leading phone companies are testing new capabilities of mobile devices with artificial intelligence. Now, these mobile devices provide information specific to the algorithms of the human mind, as well as providing recommendations to stimulate the emotions of the existing *greedy* factors in human nature. This system combined the need for information with the desire to interact with people from different parts of the world through social network platforms and created a cheap and convenient *virtual* world. The relevance of this research topic is the manipulative effect and consequences of fake traps in social networks, which have become the doors of the virtual world, on the ideology of young people.

The mobile devices we use in our daily life have brought this virtual world closer to us. According to American scientist **J.Gerald**, *"Virtual existence is an artificially created information environment, it is an information world created on the basis of various technical means, a conventional way of imagining the* *environment."*[114] **A. Smolin, D. Zhdanov, S. Potemin, V. Mezhenin, A. Bogatyrev in the educational manual "Sistemy virtualnoy, dopolnennoy i smeshannoy realyasti"** *"The virtual world contains the needs of human thinking and is designed to satisfy and direct it. For example, the social networks that we follow and interact with in our daily lives actually follow us and have almost all the realistic features about us. "Today, this network serves certain purposes and has become a center of threats,"*[115] he says. The structure of the virtual world has been extensively researched by foreign scientists J. Gerald, A. Smolin, D. Zhdanov, S. Potemin, V. Mezhenin, A. Bogatyrev, V. Temryukskom, V. G. Projerin, Y. Savchenko,[116] as well as Uzbek The research works of scientists such as G. Alimova, N. Kasimova[117] about the characteristics of social networks served as a theoretical and methodological basis for our research.

---

[114] Жералд Ж. Тхе ВР Боок: Ҳуман-Сентеред Десигн фор Виртуал Реалит. Неw Ёрк: Ассосиатион фор Сомпутинг Мачинерй анд Морган & Слайпоол, 2016. **Б.636.**

[115] Жданов Д. Д., Потемин И. С., Меженин А. В., Богатырев В.А.Системы виртуалной, дополненной и смешанной реалности : у

[116] Прожерин В.Г., Савченко Я.И. Методы распространения информатсии в соcиалных сетях // Проблема комплексного обеспечения информационной безопасности и совершенствование образовательных технологий подготовки специалистов силовых структур: Межвузовский сборник трудов В Всероссийской научно-технической конференции ИКВО НИУ ИТМО, 16-17 октября 2014 г. — 2015. **Б.335,338.**

[117] Қосимова Н.Онлайн журналистика.дарслик.Тошкент-2019. **Б.300.**

In the study, the manipulation effect and consequences of fake information threats and traps organized through virtual existence and social networks formed in it on the ideology of youth were studied based on the principles of comparative analysis.

It is known that in January 2022, the demonstrations taking place in Kazakhstan, a bordering and sister country, completely disrupted the country's government. Hundreds of people lost their lives. The fact that most of the protesters were led by the country's youth was widely discussed in all media systems. In particular, according to the information provided by State Secretary Erlan Karin to the "Tengrinews.kz" website about the situation in Kazakhstan, this demonstration and armed conflict were planned in advance by extremist organizations. He gave an interview that the dissemination of provocative information caused the rioting crowd [118] **[5.В.1].** These views were confirmed on January 18. It is natural that a question arises here: How did extremist organizations spread provocative information? The traditional method of information transmission in the process of propaganda and agitation would not have covered a large part of the audience. In particular, the majority of the citizens of the virtual world, which is called **"social media"** today, are made up of young people, and in this space there are enough opportunities to gather them, direct them, and create a conflict of opinions. In his interviews, **Erlan Karin** put forward the opinion that the cause of the armed demonstrations in the country was propaganda in social networks.

For example, it is enough to enter **two or three** keywords about the information you are looking for in the **"Google"** system on your computer or mobile device, and

---

[118] Мы столкнулись с гибридной террористической атакой -Карин. хттпс://тенгринеwс.кз/казакхстан_неwс/мйи-столкнулис-с-гибридной-террористической-атакой-карин-458614/. **Б.1.**

in a short time all the information will appear in the form of **text, audio, video, photo.** The implementation of these promotional activities in social networks is effective and happens very quickly. Let's see an example of this using the following analysis. Currently, in terms of followers, social networks **"Facebook"** and **"YouTube"** are distinguished from other networks by covering thousands of subscribers. Regarding these social networks, Vadim Lubchak, a well-known Russian journalist, said, *"The topic of manipulating the public's mind during a hybrid war is not new today. Social networks manipulate the human mind according to three main principles, i.e. **"need"**, **"interest"** and **"anticipation"** by creating an interesting thematic flow of information for the user"*.[119] For example, you only need to search three times to get the information you are interested in on social networks **Facebook** and **YouTube**, and now a daily feed of information will be sent to you automatically. Through this search system, clear lines are formed on the social network about your age, needs, interest and inclination towards information, and your psychological need for information is satisfied and you are subject to the easy information system without constantly turning to other sources. The thematic data stream forms a tape of information in audio, video and text form. It should be noted that terrorist and extremist organizations, which pose a threat to the whole world, use these networks for manipulative purposes and try to inculcate their beliefs under the guise of Islam to young people who do not have life experience and the ability to sort information. What is manipulation? **Manipulation** – this is a covert programming of the thoughts and intentions of public or individual persons, influencing their mental state, and creating attitudes and

---

[119] Вадим Лубчак.Социальные сети & манипуляции. хттпс://м.дай.кйив.уа/ру/артисле/медиа/сосиалне-сети-манипулясии. Б.2

moods to ensure behavioral reactions. The specific characteristics of the Internet (and especially social networks) allow the simultaneous use of audio, visual and textual methods in the preparation of information on a certain topic, which allows it to become the most powerful and almost the main means of influencing people (bright slogans and memorable party photos, hidden audio messages in short "25 frame method"). There are different ways to manipulate people's minds on social media. We can see manipulative technologies that look good and are easily calculated, multi-level, multi-faceted and well-thought-out and legally legitimized. M. Dzyaloshinsky emphasizes the following manipulative technologies in social networks:[120]

psychotechnology: contradictions, ridicule, suspiciously scary news headlines;

management of information flows: disclosure of "hidden information", rumors, myths;

value-emotional direction: personality or events, populism, allegory;

soliciting social support: attracting famous persons or groups, forcing propaganda;

These manipulative technologies are the most widely used methods in social networks today. So, which manipulation methods listed above do terrorist and extremist organizations use? Most of the extremist organizations collect audience on social networks **"Facebook"** and **"YouTube"** for a different purpose, and then they use 3-4 different advertising tools in this regard. The photo or video in the same thematic direction is chosen by the most supporters and the post that caused comments, and they gradually prepare their **"disciples"** by preparing manipulative psychological posts in this direction. In the course of our scientific research, we

---

[120] Дзялошинский И.М. Манипулятивные технологии в масс-медиа//Вестник Московского университета. Серия 10. Журналистика. 2005. № Б. 29.

extract data statistics from the search engine of the **Google search engine** and the search engine of the social networks **Facebook** and **YouTube** using **"hashtag keywords"** that may be used by extremists. When we entered the keyword **"Hijab"**, 31 thousand video results were found in the "Google" search engine, **70357543 in "Facebook"** and **1.7 thousand in "YouTube"**. Among these results, there are also posts of Sharia-correct educational value. However, not all youth audiences are media literate. We have only given an example of the religious dress that is popular today and has a great influence on the youth. Unfortunately, there are hundreds of Islamic words that cause this kind of controversy.

Unfortunately, today, the above-mentioned terrorist and extremist fake manipulation technologies on social networks are gradually conquering the minds of young people. Who will guarantee tomorrow that young people will not become victims of actions that they do not understand, without realizing the essence of their content?! Summarizing the ideas, the essence of the most basic technological methods of manipulation of extremist and terrorist posts in social networks:

useful interpretation of Islamic sources using reliable and reasonable arguments; For example, by distorting the verses of the Qur'an;

promotion of symbols; black dress for women, veiled hijabs, shaving for men, and materials encouraging the wearing of black.

It is well known that the problem mentioned above is related to the concepts of media knowledge of young people. In this situation, it is necessary to give medical literacy education to the child from the mother's womb. Including, in this regard, it is important to strengthen the activities of the schools of future mothers and increase the number of courses related to child upbringing.

3.2. Social networks as a key tool in preventing the spread of fake information

In 2018, according to the results of the Global social media research summary,[121] the number of Internet users reached 4.041 billion, and the number of social network users reached 3.196 billion. "In Uzbekistan, there are 20 million Internet users, and 1.6 million active users of social networks in one day".[122] About 12.1 million of the population of our republic, namely, a third of them, regularly use the Internet".[123] The majority of Internet users are students.[124]

"Nearly half of the world's population - about 3 billion people - use various social networks. The largest part of them - 2 billion people are on Facebook. According to Napoleoncat.com website, there are almost 1 million Facebook users in Uzbekistan.[125] They are on average 25-34 years old, 65.5% of them are men, 34.5% are women.

Currently, Instagram, which has an audience of 1 billion in the world, has 2,476,590 users in Uzbekistan. Facebook has united 686,400 people in our country. Telegram worth 200 million serves 18 million people in Uzbekistan.[126] Nowadays, 90 percent of young people turn to the Internet as their main source of information. Most

---

[121] O'sha yerda

[122] Абдураҳмонова С. Fake news: сохта хабарлардан қандай сақланиш мумкин?// https://kun.uz/
[123] http;//www.ziyonet.uz

[124] http;//www.ziyonet.uz

[125] Алимов Б. Ёшларнинг ижтимоий тармоклар орқали мамлакат имижини оширишдаги роли. // «Ёшлар инновацион фаоллигини оширишнинг долзарб вазифалари» мавзусидаги республика илмий-амалий коференцияси тўплами). Т., 2019. // https://beruniyalimov.uz/

[126] O'sha yerda

of the used media are social networks and video and audio portals, such as Twitter, Facebook, Odnoklasniki, YouTube. The given figures show that the World Wide Web has already become an integrated platform that has managed to attract the attention of the public, and the reliability or unreliability of its content is gaining importance day by day.

When a survey[127] was conducted to determine the purpose of using the Internet and social networks by young people, more than 100 participating students answered the question "What role do social networks on the Internet have in the lives of young people?" expressed their attitudes to the question. 30 percent of them approved the idea that these networks are necessary for making friends and making interesting acquaintances, and the same number admitted that the networks have a negative effect on the education and morals of young people. This, of course, shows that no matter how popular social networks are today, the number of people who can see their negative consequences is increasing.

"What is the role of social networks on the Internet in the lives of young people?" The results of the answers to the question were as follows:

1. Helps to make friends and make interesting acquaintances - 30 (30%);
2. Gives an opportunity to express one's opinion freely - 30 (30%);
3. It has a negative impact on youth education and morals — 20 (20%);
4. A tool for malicious persons to use for their own benefit - 10 (10%);
5. Nothing but idleness - 10 (10%).

---

[127] Ш. Раҳимова Ёшларда ахборот алмашинуви маданиятини ривожлантириш истиқболлари INFOLIB, №1, 2020 Ахборот-кутубхона журнали. https://einfolib.uz/ 13.10.2020

The fact that 10 percent of participants admitted that social networks are a tool for malicious individuals to use for their own benefit, once again indicates that Internet users do not pay attention to the truth or fakeness of the messages on it. According to the research conducted by psychologists, 15-25 percent of the population is able to critically absorb information, while the remaining 75 percent accept the received information as it is.[128]

All existing social networks influence the life of our society mainly through the activities of bloggers, influencers and other activists. Through the dissemination of information, they cause various information to be delivered to hundreds of thousands and millions of observers and contribute to the formation of public opinion about a situation of social importance.

Channels or groups on telegram and Facebook, Instagram, Odnoklasniki, Twitter, Vkontakte, etc. are sources of information dissemination since many people see or hear the information posted on these social networks,

It is known that information dissemination has its own requirements and rules established by law: calling for forceful changes to the existing constitutional system and territorial integrity of Uzbekistan, promoting war, violence, terrorism, religious extremism, separatism and fundamentalism, national, racial, ethnic or religious enmity, spreading inflammatory and other harmful information are not allowed.

"However, according to Article 29 of our Constitution, "Everyone has the right to freedom of thought, speech and belief. Everyone has the right to seek, receive and disseminate the information they want, with the exception of information directed against the current

---

[128] Полякова Т.А. Правовое обеспечение информационной безопасности при построении информационного общества в России. - Москва, 2008. – 165 с..

constitutional system and other restrictions established by law."[129]

Like all human creations, the Internet, mass media, and social networks have their own pros and cons. "Since the emergence of the Internet, some people evaluate it positively, while others talk about its negative aspects. The accepted view on this subject is that the Internet is a medium like television and radio. If we use it for good, it is good, if we use it for evil, it becomes something bad. The most important factor here is the human factor. Because a person can spread both correct information and bad information at the same time"[130].

According to statistics, "the number of fake materials published in 2018 increased by 32%. This means that people's trust in official sources of information has dropped to 32%. Fake news has a lot in common with the yellow press and political propaganda. But it is possible to distinguish a fake from artistic textures and rumors. Since the rumors in the yellow press are spread mainly to waste the public's time, to draw attention to one or another person, its social damage is not very significant. Fakes are dangerous because they are false news that are spread for socio-political purposes or financial gain. You can be sure of this from the examples given below".

"April 16, 2021"

"Warning: Scammers are operating on the Internet in the name of the Cyber Crime Unit

On the Internet, on behalf of the cyber crime department of the Ministry of Internal Affairs of the Republic of Uzbekistan, citizens are told that it is

---

[129] Блогерларнинг қандай ҳуқуқлари бор? Мажбуриятлари-чи?// https://teletype.in/. 08.12.1992. Ўзбекистон Республикасининг Конституцияси (lex.uz)

[130] Блогерларнинг қандай ҳуқуқлари бор? Мажбуриятлари-чи?// https://teletype.in/. 08.12.1992. Ўзбекистон Республикасининг Конституцияси (lex.uz)

necessary to transfer money to a bank card in the amount of 240,000 sums in order to fight against "elements that distribute various prohibited materials, including those that promote violence, cruelty and contain pornography," etc.

Dear citizens! Please be critical of these types of posts. Internal affairs bodies do not ask citizens to make money transfers to any account! We will officially announce it.

If you receive a notice of this nature, please report it to the nearest internal affairs department. This will be your biggest contribution to the fight against cybercrime.

Information Service of the Ministry of Internal Affairs".[131]

Or another example:

Uzbeks are being cheated with a fake "Telegram premium" subscription

Fraudsters started sending messages in mass on social networks.

It offers a reward in the form of a free Telegram premium subscription.

Be careful not to click on the link in the bot! Otherwise, you may lose your Telegram account and personal data.

---

[131] https://iiv.uz/oz/news/2021, 16-aprel.

Today, most of our compatriots managed to fall into this trap. Now their accounts are also sending trap messages to their acquaintances. Be careful!"[132]

Another example:

Cybersecurity Center warns

Messages under the title "One-time financial aid to citizens" are being distributed on various channels and groups through the Telegram messenger.

Don't believe the news about "social payment of 400,000 soums for each family due to the increase of unemployment in the country, as well as many social problems", which is distributed using the official website of the President of the Republic of Uzbekistan. The Cyber Security Center of the Ministry of Internal Affairs warns that these reports are false.

It is noted that fraudsters are trying to distribute the link to others in the Telegram messenger through users.

"Be careful not to fall into the trap of Internet scammers"[133]

As can be seen from the examples given above, "modern information technologies create many conveniences and opportunities in the life of society, but also cause some problems. In most cases, these problems

---

[132] https://sangzor.uz/mediasavodxonlik/ 2022, 17-noyabr.

[133] https://sangzor.uz/mediasavodxonlik/

arise as a result of malicious use of information **communication** tools and their capabilities."[134]

In such a situation, it becomes a mega-important necessity to protect against fake, fake or information threatening social security at the state level. At the same time, it is necessary to remember that information is a national wealth for any country, and "a strategic resource in the international arena."[135] Because, "In the 20th century, nuclear weapons posed a threat to humanity, but by the 21st century, information attacks organized under the guise of religion for various purposes are endangering the whole world."[136] In the era of globalization, there is an unprecedented struggle to win the hearts and minds of young people.

Taking over the opponent's information space, discrediting his identity, destabilizing his life is the main goal of an information attack.

The term "information attack" was first mentioned in 1976 in Thomas Rohn's report "Weapons System and Information Warfare" for Boeing.[137] It is noted that an important aspect of an information attack is "the ability to put psychological pressure on the leaders and members of the enterprises of the opposing country and force them to make the necessary decisions."

An information attack is an attempt to shape social facts and public consciousness in a desired direction by

---

[134] www.jizzax.uz. Исматов Э. Энг хавфли хуруж бу ахборот хуружидир.// , 2020, 25 апрель.

[135] Oʻsha manba

[136] Маматкулов А.А. ўкувчи- ёшлар ўртасида интернет ва ижтимоий тармоқлардан фойдаланиш маданиятини шакллантириш.// Замонавий таълим / Современное образование 2020, 6 (91).).

[137] Oʻsha manba

exerting pressure on a rival person, society or state from the political, economic, social and cultural spheres. In the implementation of information attacks, the enemy mainly uses disinformation, manipulation, propaganda, incitement, slander, discrediting, making noises to attract public attention (using true and false information), spreading rumors, conspiracy, uses methods such as crisis management. These factors are detailed in the first chapter.

At the current stage, mass media and information and communication technologies are used as the main means to achieve the goal. The "syndrome" of disseminating fake and false news mainly "breaks out" on the eve of important political events, around topics that are causing great resonance these days. The influence of fakes on the human mind can be seen from the following data: after the US presidential election in December 2016, 64 percent of respondents stated that their opinion about reality was confused due to fake news, 24 percent of respondents were not sure that their election choices were correct, and 23 percent of respondents were conscious or they noted that they unconsciously participated in spreading false news.[138]

The most damaging feature of fakes is their ability to reproduce themselves. That is, they suddenly get rich with false details, mislead and mislead people. The main purpose of a fake is to manipulate public opinion.

The proliferation of fake information in this way can lead to the loss of the reputation of some individuals and the emergence of panic in society. Also, fakes damage the reputation of mass media and create distrust towards them. Therefore, both the mass media and each person should be protected from fakes themselves or their distribution. For this, it is necessary to identify a fake or conduct a **Fact-check**. Fact-checking means analyzing facts. By comparing the discrepancies between existing

---

[138] Абдураҳмонова С. Fake news: сохта хабарлардан қандай сақланиш мумкин?// https://kun.uz/ 25 апрель

facts and reality, the truth or falsity of the facts is determined.

Fact-checking requires a thorough study of the source, reading the message to the end, checking the author, links, dates, being impartial in receiving information, studying the opinion of experts, going from the message to the home page, and studying the purpose, tasks and content of the site.

The use of auxiliary resources is also required to detect fakes. By uploading a photo to the Tinee service, it is possible to find the original photo, its different size options, when it was uploaded to the network, and also find information about computer processing.

When detecting a fake video on YouTube, it is passed through the YouTube DataViewer service, where it is possible to see the time the video was uploaded to the network and screenshots.

You can get complete information about videos uploaded from different platforms from the InVID service. It can show the "path" of the video from the time it was uploaded to the Internet, whether it has been processed or not.

To date, no country has developed a single comprehensive sequence of measures against the methods of information attacks. In our opinion, the main reasons for this are the speed of information and communication technologies, the fact that they do not know borders, do not choose a nationality, and are developing at a very fast pace.

In conclusion, it can be said that in order to resist the growing ideological, ideological and informational threat in the modern international information space, it is necessary to organize spiritual and educational activities in accordance with the needs of the times, to protect the population and especially young people from ideological attacks, to distinguish whether the information is true or false at the first reading. education, formation of media literacy and information culture in them, development of the national information space while preventing the lack of information in society, correct and impartial assessment of events, putting an end to the subversive actions of destructive forces, fighting against various foreign ideas, and training mature specialists for this field are required . .

There is currently no specific information or advice on how social media can help detect and prevent fakes. Facebook has tried some anti-fake measures, but these have also been ineffective.

3.3. Fact- checking as an element of media literacy

Media literacy teaches you to distinguish fake news from real ones. In order to distinguish a real fact from a fake, as we mentioned in the first chapter, it is necessary to have a critical approach to information, to analyze the received information, to compare it with other sources, and to be able to draw independent conclusions about it. Conclusions are required to be based on good faith, experience and knowledge. It was mentioned in the first chapter.

Today, the development of media literacy, which is an integral part of modern media education, is determined not by the improvement of information technologies, but by the increase of new scientific and educational information sources. "We can add to the list of positive aspects of information exchange that young people can rationally use scientific and educational resources such as MySQL, EBSCO, eLibrary, JSTOR, ProQues, Emerald."[139]

In the process of modernization of society, the culture of information exchange among the country's youth shows a trend of stable development. It shows that it is a vital necessity to conduct a step-by-step sociological study of the culture of information exchange and the productive and systematic use of information among our

---

[139] Раҳимова Ш. Ёшларда ахборот алмашинуви маданиятини ривожлантириш истиқболлари// INFOLIB, №1, 2020. Ахборот-кутубхона журнали https://einfolib.uz/

youth, to develop effective ways and means of solving the problem, and to give suggestions and recommendations.

The purpose of a person to turn to this or that information channel is understandable. The selection is based on the completeness of the message, the credibility or interest of the source, etc. But even here it is necessary to study the reliability of the source in depth.

So, based on the selection of information, its value lies to the consumer, even if he does not understand it. When evaluating a source of information, first of all, it is necessary to determine the purpose of receiving information from it, and to be able to determine which source is the most reliable for obtaining information, and which sources can be truthful and unbiased. Such a process helps to identify reliable sources of information.

A source of information is usually a person or information carrier who has information of social importance (that is, of interest and need to the general public).

Today, when it comes to the development of media literacy among the masses, many experts in the field began to pay special attention to the experience of Finland, which was recognized at the international conference on media literacy held in Almaty on June 9-10. Dr. Lauri Palsa, Senior Adviser on Media Literacy at the Finnish Ministry of Education's National Institute of Audiovisual Media, in his public lecture entitled **"Towards Sustainable Structures in the Digital Age: Development of Public Media Literacy Policy"** recognizes the following about media literacy: "Media literacy is a key enabler of cultural, social and democratic participation in society . "Media literacy skills provide protection, good work, well-being and are a guarantee of national security."[140] The speaker said that the National Institute of Audiovisual Media coordinates the

---

[140] Махмудов Н. Медиасаводхонлик қандай тарғиб қилинади? Финлландия тажрибаси https://newreporter.org/uz/2022/06/30/

development of media literacy by supporting organizations and individuals who contribute to the development of media literacy in Finland, which has become one of the leading countries in terms of media literacy both in Europe and in the world.

According to the speaker, Finnish media education policy has a long tradition. In the 70s of the last century, the state allocated a lot of money for the development of the country's education system. First of all, the Finns tried to turn schools into small communities (there are no big schools in the country: the number of students in all schools is on average around 300, and the number of students in each class does not exceed 20), and to achieve this, its builders paid great attention to the training of teachers. A total of 5-year teacher training program consisting of three-year bachelor's degree and two-year master's degree was introduced, and a master's degree was made mandatory to become a teacher.

The most difficult admission to the pedagogy course has been introduced, and only 10% of applicants can pass the test. That is, it is not a field that one enters by hand because one does not know where to apply, but one of the most prestigious fields, such as the legal or economic field. From this point of view, Finnish teachers are highly qualified and take strong responsibility for their work, in turn, high trust and respect for teachers has been formed in the society.

As a result of 30-40 years of continuous training of extremely high-level teachers in Finland, all schools in the country are filled with elite-level teachers. Therefore, teaching has become one of the prestigious professions in Finnish society. Their salary is on average 2900 to 3600 euros.[141] Many young people aspire to this profession.

Funds invested in education in an unfavorable climate, achieved its status with great difficulties (Finland,

---

[141] https://zagranportal.ru/finliandia/rabota Трудоустройство в Финляндии в 2022 году: на какую зарплату можно рассчитывать?

which was a colony of Sweden for a long time, then became an autonomous part of the Russian Empire, and gained independence by 1917. Later, in order to preserve this independence, in the wars with the USSR, Finland lost 10% of its territory and about 100,000 people. sacrificed a soldier, and also conducted its foreign policy with the permission of the USSR (in exchange for maintaining its internal independence, unlike the countries of Central and Eastern Europe) has now become one of the most advanced countries in the world. The country's long history of colonization is evident from the pictures: Helsinki is hard to distinguish from St. Petersburg or Polish cities at first glance) [142] which transformed the country from a poor country to one with a strong economy and a high standard of living. Systematic media education in schools also began in the 1970s. The first national media literacy policy was adopted in 2013. The previous policy was completed in 2016, and the Ministry of Education and Culture entrusted the process of finalizing the new policy to the National Audiovisual Institute in 2019. In international studies on the assessment of the quality of education, the Finnish education system was recognized as the most advanced in all respects. In the "Media and Information Literacy" study, Denmark and Finland were noted as the most advanced countries in Europe, where media literacy is closely linked to national policies and the concept of human rights and active citizenship.

Finnish students have by far achieved the best results in terms of quality of education.

The Finnish Basic Education Act (1998) defines three main goals of Finnish education:

1. *To give students the knowledge and skills they need in life;*

---

[142] Финляндия қандай қилиб дунёдаги энг яхши таълим тизимига эга бўлди?// https://zamin.uz/dunyo/ 2014-2022 «Zamin» - Ўзбекистон янгиликлари..

2. *Promotion of development and equality in society and;*
3. *Ensuring equality in education throughout the country.*

Five days of study per week have been introduced in schools. All schools have the same status, children are not separated into different classes or specialized educational institutions according to their abilities. Equality is the most basic principle in the education system, as in all areas of society.

Primary education in Finnish schools lasts for 6 years and children are not graded until the 3rd grade, teachers hardly give homework,

In Finland, media literacy is promoted and supported through high-quality, systematic and comprehensive media education, probably because all schools have "gone pen-less" in class since 2017 and are fully using computers and tablets in the classroom.

Comprehensive media education refers to an overview of the content, perspectives, target groups and geographical distribution of media education provided in Finland.

Quality media education is developed, developed and evaluated based on various studies.

Systematic media education means that media education provided in Finland is systematic and consistent. In Finland, media education is available in all educational institutions, both formal and informal. Media education is used at the level of preschool education, schools, libraries, youth organizations, museums, state and public organizations, non-governmental non-profit organizations, national, regional and local companies.

The scope of media education can be wide and varied. Media education can be promoted, taught, developed and implemented at different levels. The general education system provides the basis for media education, as it gives everyone equal access to this knowledge. Media education covers administrative areas such as education and culture, transport and communications, social issues and health. In the implementation of the media literacy policy, the main attention is paid to the various needs of people, and the most necessary and optimal measures and actions are selected to satisfy them.

In Finland, mmedia literacy opportunities for everyone have been improved and this is being promoted under the slogan "Mmedia literacy for all". Media literacy, which contributes to a good, meaningful lifestyle, is an important element of citizenship.

Doctor Lauri Palsa

When developing a media literacy policy, it should be remembered that its scope, goals and perspectives will be different. For example, media literacy policies are found in international and national forms. Media literacy policies can be part of the curriculum as well as the national curriculum. Media literacy can be seen across sectors, such as media literacy in libraries, education and youth work. There may also be media literacy policies at the regional level. Therefore, media literacy is promoted, including at the municipal level, in various forms, such as research, surveys, interviews, site development, consultations.

Developing countries should pay close attention to one aspect of Finland's experience, that is, if something needs to be learned, it should be based not on the current state of the Finnish education system, but on the state of the Finnish education system 50-60 years ago and what steps were taken to solve the problems of those times. We should take into account that we are in "that situation"[143] now.

1. Where do you get most of your information?

According to the results of this survey, 28 percent of students answered that through mass media, and 72 percent of students answered that through the Internet. According to the results of the final summary, it is convenient and fast to get information from the Internet for most students.

---

[143] https://zamin.uz/dunyo 14.02.2020 **Финляндия қандай қилиб дунёдаги энг яхши таълим тизимига эга бўлди?**

1. Сиз ахборотни кўпроқ қаердан оласиз?

1. ***https://docs.google.com/forms/d/1uepxrLm_CIqrFja0BSX eMMGm8PRG1Xjf0palRrG5c8/edit***

In particular, it is the conduct of "informational hours" within the framework of coaching hours in higher education institutions. Important events published in the media will be discussed with the students, comments will be made on the transmitted information, and the news image of today will be observed.

Today, in order to determine the audience's channels for receiving information, we determined the most watched information network on the Internet platform by conducting the following survey.

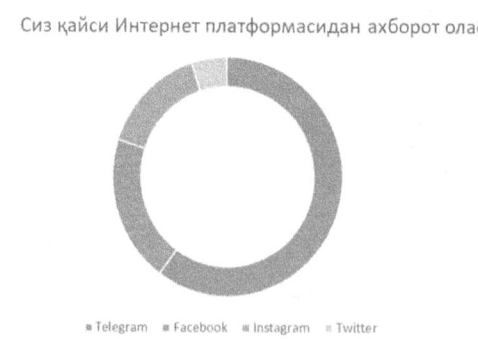

2. From which Internet platform do you get information? According to the results of the survey conducted in the "Talented Students of the Republic" club, today 60 percent of students consider it

preferable to receive information from Telegram, 20 percent from Facebook, 15 percent from Instagram, and 5 percent from Twitter.

3. Check your media literacy by commenting on the following post?

"Russia has become the first country in the world to perform an autopsy on a COVID-19 corpse. After a thorough investigation, he determined that COVID-19 does not exist as a virus, but rather a bacterium that has been exposed to radiation and causes death through blood clotting.

COVID-19 has been found to cause blood clotting, which causes thrombosis in humans and causes blood to clot in the veins, making it difficult for the brain, heart, and lungs to breathe, causing rapid death in humans.

To find the cause of the lack of respiratory energy, doctors in Russia defy WHO protocol and perform a COVID-19 autopsy. After the doctors opened the arms, legs and other parts of the body and carefully examined them, they noticed that the blood vessels were dilated and filled with blood clots, which often obstructed the flow of blood and also reduced the flow of oxygen. in the body it causes the death of the patient. Upon learning of this study, the Russian Ministry of Health immediately changed its COVID-19 treatment protocol and prescribed aspirin to positive patients. 100 mg and started taking Empromac. As a result, patients began to recover and their health began to improve. The Ministry of Health of Russia discharged more than 14,000 patients in one day and sent them home.

Doctors in Russia explained the treatment after several scientific discoveries, stating that this disease is a worldwide lie, "it is nothing more than an intra-vascular blood clot (thrombosis) and the treatment is curative." Take Antibiotic Pills, Anti-Inflammatories and Anticoagulants (aspirin). This shows that the disease is treatable. According to other Russian scientists, ventilators and an intensive care unit were never needed. Protocols on this have already been published in Russia

The Chinese government already knew about it, but never released its report. Share this information with your family, neighbors, acquaintances, friends, colleagues, so they can get rid of the fear of COVID-19 and understand that it is not a virus, but only a bacterium exposed to 5G radiation. Only use caution in people with very low immune systems. This radiation also causes inflammation and hypoxia. Victims should take Asprin 100 mg and Apronic or Paracetamol 650 mg.

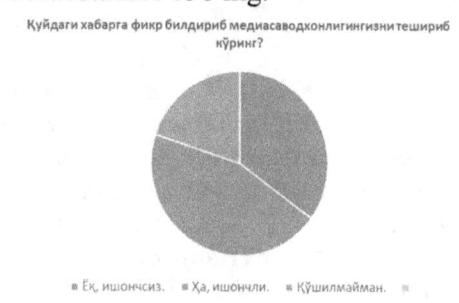

https://docs.google.com/forms/d/1uepxrLm_CIqrFja0BSXeMMGm8PRG1Xjf0palRrG5c8/edit

According to the results of the survey conducted among the activists of the "Talented Students-Youths of the Republic" club, 20 percent of students disagreed with whether the news was reliable or not, 45 percent accepted the news as reliable, and 35 percent of media-literate students approved the news's unreliability. Therefore, the role of media education in improving media literacy is very important. Including, it is necessary to form specific knowledge skills in students regarding the concepts of "mmedia literacy" and "media education".

Tashkent Institute of Chemical Technology, Yangiyer branch, between January and February 2023, we organized a questionnaire consisting of 7 questions in order to determine the level of media literacy of students on the telegram channel "TKT Yangiyer filiali.uz". Today, the number of followers on this site is 15,664. Most of the active users are teachers and students. Average daily tracking results are 6,690. 1,300 observers actively participated in the survey that we provided as part of our research. Since 300 observers did not provide answers to the questionnaire within the requirement, we included the total active audience layer as 1000.

In the age group, 18-25-year-olds make up the main part - 81.7 percent. 16-18-year-olds accounted for 7.2 percent, 25-30-year-olds for 10.7 percent, and over 30-year-olds for 2.4 percent.

Table 1.

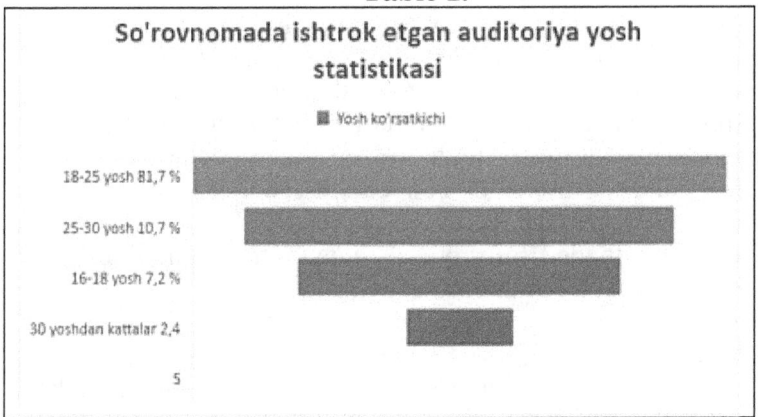

One of the main questions following the screening questions, the question "You get information from a social network or from which internet platform", is intended to determine the audience's relationship with the source of information, the media. To this question, 64% of respondents reported that they follow information sources transmitted through Telegram, 25% of Facebook, and 11% of Instagram.

Table 2.

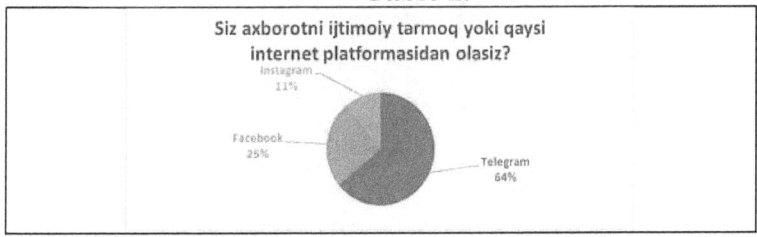

Today, the volume of messages transmitted through "Telegram" is significant for a large part of the audience. Because today this platform is a leading tool in the state system and has a fast flow of information. The social network "Facebook" is mainly reminiscent of opinion journalism. It can be said that through this network, users have become a forum for sharing their attitude towards the events of today. According to the opinion of most observers, it is possible to find out the world and local news that are causing the most urgent discussion using this social network. Instagram is a virtual entertainment place for followers with its fun and popular best video feed and a number of convenient features. According to the lowest percentage in the survey, this social network is mainly intended for cultural recreation and entertainment rather than information.

In order to check the knowledge of students and young people about the concept of fake and disinformation in today's media space, the survey asked "What is a fake?" 33% of respondents answered "false information" to our question. Also, 65% of the respondents gave the concept of "falsified news" as a fake, while 2% of the participants answered that it was a true news.

Table 3.

Feyk nima?

- Yolg'on axborot — 32%
- Soxtalashtirilgan xabar — 63%
- To'g'ri xabar — 5%

Based on this question, it can be noted that students do not have sufficient knowledge and skills regarding the meaning of the concepts of fake and disinformation.

"How do you spot fake news?" to the question, 58% of respondents answered "through fact-checking instruments", 39% of participants said "from reliable sites" and 3% of respondents "don't care".

Table 4.

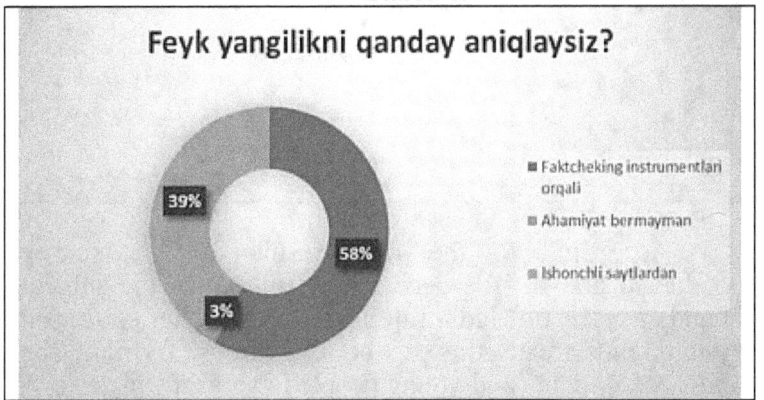

This question was organized in order to study the knowledge of students and young people about the methods of identifying fake news, and according to the final results, the competence in identifying fake news was well formed.

"Where do you look for the right information?" to our next question, 78% of respondents said that they search from "media", 12% from "messengers" and 10% of participants said that they search from "social networks". The fact that a large part of the audience receives information through social networks indicates the need to understand the role of social networks in disseminating information and polarizing political opinion, and to acquire digital skills based on critical thinking. Caroline Tagg, Philip Seargeant examines the impact of social media on the case of Facebook, and the social or interpersonal nature of modern Internet use must be taken into account when dealing with disinformation and political polarization.

Table 5.

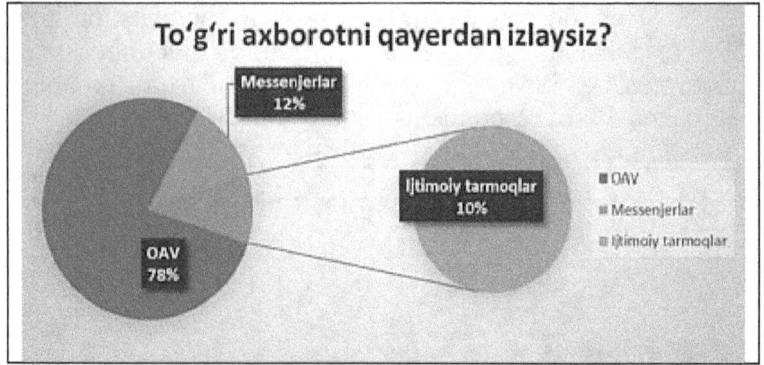

According to the final results of the survey conducted above, it is necessary to introduce the subject "Fundamentals of Media Literacy" in the higher education system and create this textbook, thereby forming the ability of students and young people to sort information.

Conclusion
According to the results of the conducted research, we came to the following conclusions:
1. The emergence and rapid development of the information society led to a sharp change in the political, economic and socio-cultural landscape of the world. The introduction of information and communication technologies on a global scale has made it possible to rapidly increase the flow of information and to influence individual and social consciousness through them. Managing the post-industrial society with the power of information and mass media has become crucial. For this reason, reliable and safe operation of world mass information and mass communication systems has become an urgent issue on the agenda.
2. The mass media, which is a subsystem of mass media, has the most significant impact on social consciousness. They use direct and indirect methods of influencing public opinion. Media practice is the most used of these methods to manipulate the human mind and provide the population with false information.
3. Due to the fact that the Internet, especially social networks, has become a convenient and safe place for the spread of "fake news" and disinformation, it is necessary to check the facts covered by the mass media and the content of social networks, to increase the media literacy of journalists and bloggers, to fight against online violence in the fight against fake and false information. fighting has become an urgent problem waiting for its solution in the field of information. If these issues are not resolved in the near future and if the current situation in the formation of world information civilization remains a stable trend, the information war may become the main weapon in the hands of the initiators and leaders of the information society. At the same time, they have been able to achieve information superiority in certain social systems, in changing the direction of mass public activity and controlling the change of public consciousness through

mass media. The main goal of information warfare is to achieve this value.

4. While information and communication technologies provide instant access to vast reserves of information and knowledge, information providers such as mass media, libraries, archives, and the Internet provide a new type of service. That is, new generation technologies provide opportunities to quickly and efficiently meet the needs of education, research, meaningful spending of free time, as well as integration of different communities. At the same time, the media and other sources of information provide leadership in mass information and communication processes.

5. Mass media and information literacy have already become the demand of the time. Media literacy requires the ability to critically approach any (true and false) information, analyze it, compare it with other sources, make comparisons, and draw independent conclusions about it. Such skills are essential for countering or preventing modern information wars and information attacks. Finland's experience in media literacy education is considered exemplary.

6. Media literacy alone is not enough to fight fakes and disinformation. It is necessary to hold the disseminators of destructive information, who bring chaos to the society, to legal responsibility, to put an end to their activities, and to widely promote the advanced legal experiences accumulated in the world in this regard. After all, although serious measures and measures against the spread of fake information are being taken in many countries of the world, they have not yet brought the expected results.

7. In the Republic of Uzbekistan, appropriate legal and regulatory documents and special decisions against the dissemination of false information and disinformation have been adopted, and this extremely negative process is strictly controlled by law enforcement agencies, but the spread of fake information is observed in the mass media and various social networks. In order to prevent the flow

of fake and false information, the need to adopt a special law and improve the existing legislation has become an urgent demand of the time.

8. In the process of modernization of the society of Uzbekistan, it is necessary to improve the culture of information exchange among young people and the conditions of efficient and systematic use of information, in which it is necessary to consistently study the current situation through sociological research.

We found it necessary to give the following recommendations for the solution of the scientific problem posed in this study:

1. When the user's page was opened on the social network, it must be checked when this was opened. Sometimes new accounts are created to spread disinformation and mystification. One of the useful features of Twitter is that it shows when a new profile design is launched.

2. It is necessary to study the activity of the user. With whom is he a friend?

made friends, who do they correspond with, who did they add to their profile, what does they write about, what does they talk about? A social network provides a wealth of information about human interactions and influences.

3. It is necessary to search for other social network accounts of the user. On which other pages of the Internet can the name of the person you are looking for be found? It is necessary to use Spokeo, Pipl.com to search for it. WebMii and Linkedin should try to get phone number, address and other information.

4. Contacting the person who downloaded and published the news is very important check. It is necessary to obtain additional information and to find out what requirements are set for the material, to check whether it is possible to obtain permission to use the information.

5. Research by image should be used. Note it is said that a recent photo can often appear to be an old photo. You can use Google Reverse Image Search or Tinee to check this. You'll see this image appear on the web. This

feature also works for video thumbnails - the search engine will tell you where else you can see it.

6. It is also important to check the photo details. Every digital image has metadata that tells you what you can't see. Among other useful information, EXIF can help identify the type of camera that took the shot. Geographic information is sometimes written.

SUGGESTIONS

First, it is necessary to develop a plan of measures in our country at the same time when the flow of global information is increasing, as well as to form a culture of information sorting.

Secondly, in the fight against fake and disinformation, it is necessary to determine the tasks of media literacy and gradually develop it in the educational system.

Thirdly, it is important to set the main task of increasing media literacy by organizing educational textbooks and courses to expand the scope of scientific research in a systematic fight against fakes and disinformation.

Fourthly, since fake verbal and non-verbal information poses a great threat to society and people's lives, it is necessary to fight against it on an international scale and to organize international scientific and practical conferences among researchers.

Fifth, it is necessary to organize seminars and trainings in order to further improve the knowledge and skills of instrumental sorting of fake and disinformation information in educational institutions.

Sixthly, it is necessary to introduce the subject "Fundamentals of Media Education" included in the three-year curriculum based on world experience in improving student media literacy. In this subject, in turn, it is necessary to strengthen practical lessons with foreign experience while conducting practical training.

The general constructive mechanism of theoretical and practical training for one academic year within the framework of the "Basics of Media Education" subject:

For 1st courses. Analysis of the psychological significance of means of communication, information and its types in the information society;

For 2nd courses. Analysis of press, radio, TV and online publications of international strategic importance in the media space;

For 3 courses. Types of media products in online publications and their psycholinguistic characteristics.

First, students receive theoretical knowledge within the framework of the "Fundamentals of Media Education" subject during half-yearly training sessions. In the second semester of practical training, they will find psychologically important journalistic materials and analyze them on the example of national and international experience. In order to further strengthen theoretical knowledge, it will be strengthened by conducting seminars and trainings with powerful journalists of the CIS countries. This system serves as a foundation for strengthening media literacy skills of future personnel through media education. Personnel with the necessary knowledge will serve to increase the information consumption culture of the audience during their future activities.

LIST OF REFERENCES

1. Legal and regulatory documents
1. Oʻzbekiston Respublikasining Konstitusiyasi. – T.: Oʻzbekiston. 2017.
2. Oʻzbekiston Respublikasi Prezidentining 2017-yil 7-fevraldagi "Oʻzbekiston Respublikasini yanada rivojlantirish boʻyicha Harakatlar strategiyasi toʻgʻrisida"gi PF-4947-sonli Farmoni. Oʻzbekiston Respublikasi qonun hujjatlari toʻplami, 2017. №6. 70-modda.
3. Oʻzbekiston Respublikasi Prezidentining 2017-yil 11-avgustdagi "Matbuot va axborot sohasida boshqaruvni yanada takomillashtirish toʻgʻrisida"gi PF-5148-sonli Farmoni. www.lex.uz
5. Oʻzbekiston Respublikasida ommaviy axborot vositalari faoliyati, rivojlanish, erkinligi kafolatlari toʻgʻrisidagi tahliliy ma'lumot. (OʻzMAA. 2013-yil, 1 iyun). www.infoCOM.UZ.
6. Oʻzbekiston Respublikasi Vazirlar Mahkamasining "Oʻzbekiston Respublikasining umumta'lim muassasalarida "Mediata'lim" oʻquv dasturini ishlab chiqish va tatbiq etish toʻgʻrisida"gi Farmoyishi. Xalq soʻzi, 2012-yil. 18-dekabr soni.

2. Works of the President of the Republic of Uzbekistan
1. Mirziyoyev Sh. M. Erkin va farovon, demokratik Oʻzbekiston davlatini birgalikda barpo etamiz. – Toshkent: "Oʻzbekiston" NMIU, 2016.
2. Mirziyoyev Sh..Milliy taraqqiyot yoʻlimizni qat'iyat bilan davom ettirib yangi bosqichga koʻtaramiz". T.1. –T.: "Oʻzbekiston", 2017-yil.
3. Mirziyoyev Sh. "Xalqimizning roziligi bizning faoliyatimizga berilgan eng oliy bahodir". T.2. –T.: "Oʻzbekiston", 2018-yil.
4. Mirziyoyev Sh. "Niyati ulugʻ xalqning ishi ham ulugʻ, hayoti yorugʻ va kelajagi farovon boʻladi". T.3. – T.: "Oʻzbekiston", 2018-yil.

3. Books and serial publications

1. Абдураҳмонова С. Fake news: сохта хабарлардан қандай сақланиш мумкин?// https://kun.uz/

2. Алимов Б. Ёшларнинг ижтимоий тармоклар орқали мамлакат имижини оширишдаги роли. // «Ёшлар инновацион фаоллигини оширишнинг долзарб вазифалари» мавзусидаги республика илмий-амалий коференцияси тўплами). Т., 2019. // https://beruniyalimov.uz/

3. Аҳмедов Т. Ўзбекистонда экстремизмга қарши кураш борасидаги ёндашувлар концептуал жиҳатдан ўзгармоқда- 06.04.2021// https://nuz.uz/uz/zhamoat/

4. Болотнов А. В. Информационные волны и их типы в современном медиадискурсе: к постановке проблемы. // Вестник ТГПУ (TSPU Bulletin). 2015.

5. Блогерларнинг қандай ҳуқуқлари бор? Мажбуриятлари-чи?// https://teletype.in/. 08.12.1992. Ўзбекистон Республикасининг Конституцияси (lex.uz).

6. В Латвии возбудили дело за распространение фейков о коронавирусе [Электронный ресурс] // РИА «Новости». URL: https://ria.ru/20200201/1564132102.html (дата обращения: 25.02.2020)

7. Винькеле: Латвия полностью готова к встрече с коронавирусом [Электронный ресурс] // Новостное агентство "Sputnik". URL: https://lv.sputniknews.ru/Latvia/20200210/13195694/Vinkele-Latviya-polnostyu-gotova-k-vstreche-s-koronavirusom.html.

8. Воронова О.Е. Трушин А. С. .Функции фейков в современных информационных войнах.// https://histrf.ru/magazine/article/

9. Глава ВОЗ призвал бороться с дезинформацией в связи со вспышкой коронавируса [Электронный ресурс] // Информационное агентство «ТАСС». URL: https

10. Гридчин А.А. Коммуникативные технологии регулирования региональных конфликтов // Вестник Волгоградского государственного университета. Серия 7: Философия, социология и социальные технологии. Волгоград, 2009. № 1 (9).

11. Дўстмуҳаммад Х. "Оммавий ахборот воситаларини ривожлантиришнинг демократик андозалари" Т., "Ўзбекистон"- 2005.

12. Дўстмуҳаммад Х. Ахборот мўъжиза, жозиба, фалсафа, Т.: "Янги аср авлоди" 2013.

13. Ёкубова О. Ўзбекистоннинг диний экстремизм ва халқаро терроризмга қарши глобал курашдаги ўрни https://savollar.muslimaat.uz/

14. Жаботинская С. Исследователи определили семь типов фейковых новостей.// https://naked-science.ru/article/media/issledovateli-opredelili-sem-tipov-fejkovyh-novostej

15. Зырянова М.О. Способы противодействия распространению фейковой информации.// cyberleninka.ru.

16. Ижтимоий тармоқлардаги экстремистик ва террористик деб топилган саҳифалар рўйхати янгиланди. // Янгиликларимиз халқ учун. https://www.gazeta.uz/uz/2022/01/25.

17. Ильченко С. Н. Как нас обманывают СМИ: манипуляция информацией. СПб.: Питер, 2019.

18. Ирназаров К.Т., Маматова Я.М. Информация в печати (Краткий курс лекций). – Т.: НУУз, 2000.

19. Иссерс О. Медиафейки: между правдой и мистификацией // Коммуникативные исследования. 2014. № 2.

20. Ищенкова М. С. Проблемы привлечения к уголовной ответственности при осуществлении экстремистской деятельности в сети Интернет. // http://www.ling-expert.ru/conference/

21. Исматов Э. Энг хавфли хуруж бу ахборот хуружидир.// www.jizzax.uz. 25 апрель 2020 йил.

22. Каримов. И.А. Юксам маънавият – енгидмас куч. Маънавият нашриёти – 2008.

23. Комиссаров М. А. "Проблема распространения недостоверной информации в СМИ и социальных медиа"// Тезисы к выступлению на 20-й Центрально-Азиатской Конференции СМИ "Будущее журналистики". https://www.osce.org/representative-on-freedom-ofmedia.

24. Королева О. Сиз нима учун медиа саводли бўлишингиз керак? (Курбонбоева Ш. Таржимаси)// https://newreporter.org/uz/author/shahnoza/

25. Королько В.Г. Основы паблик релейшнз. М.,. 343 б. Зырянова М.О. Способы противодействия распространению фейковой информации.// cyberleninka.ru. 2000.

26. Лебедева Е.Г. Фейковые новости как инструмент манипулятивного воздействия в медиасреде // Universum: филология и искусствоведение : электрон. научн. журн. 2021. 3(81).

URL: https://7universum.com/ru/philology/archive/item/11340 .

27. Маматова Я.М., Сулайманова С.Н. Ўзбекистон медиатаълим тараққиёти йўлида. Ўқув қўлланма.–Т.: «Extremum-press», 2015.

28. Маматова Я.М. Арифханова С.Н. Зўравон экстремизмнинг олдини олиш масалалари: массмедиада ёритиш (ўқув қўлланма) Т., «Vneshinvestprom» 2020.

29. Маматкулов А.А. Ўқувчи- ёшлар ўртасида интернет ва ижтимоий тармоқлардан фойдаланиш маданиятини шакллантириш.// Замонавий таълим / Современное образование 2020.

30. Манойло А. В. «Фейковые новости» как метод перехвата нформационной повестки в условиях современного информационного противоборства // Культурная политика. 2019. № 1. Официальный сайт «История.рф». URL: https://histrf.ru/magazine/release

31. Махмудов Н. Медиасаводхонлик қандай тарғиб қилинади? Финнляндия тажрибаси https://newreporter.org/uz/2022/06/30/

32. Медиа ва ахборот саводхонлиги Педагоглар учун методик қўлланма Тузувчилар: Б. Намазов, М. Файзиева, Ғ. Джалилов. Baktria press Тошкент – 2018.

33. Медиа ва ахборот саводхонлиги Ўқув қўлланма Тузувчилар: Б. Намазов, М. Файзиева, Ш. Шарофаддинов.

34. Медиа саводхонлик бўйича халқаро конференцияда МАСни тарғиб қилишнинг миллий стратегиялари таклиф қилинди | Янги репортер (newreporter.org).

35. Молина М. Д., Сундар С. Ш., Тай Ле, Донгвон Ли. «Фейковые новости» — это не просто ложная информация: концепция экспликации и таксономии онлайн-контента. journals.sagepub.com/doi/full/10.1177/0002764219878224

36. Муротова Н.Ф, Тошпўлатова Н.К., Алимова Г.Б. fake news: медиада дезинформация Журналистика ва коммуникация йўналишлари талабалари учун қўлланма. Тошкент – "Инновацион ривожланиш нашриёт-матбаа уйи" – 2020.

37. Назайкин А.Н. «Современное медиапланирование. Учебное пособие». Солон-пресс, 2016 г. ISBN: 978-5-91359-210-1.

38. Павликова М.М. Парадоксы информационого общества. Вестник МГУ, серия 10.Журналистика.- №1. 2008.

39. Полякова Т.А. Правовое обеспечение информационной безопасности при построении информационного общества в России. - Москва, 2008.

40. Почепцов Г.Г. Информационные войны. М., 2001.

41. Распопова С. С., Богдан Е. Н. Фейковые новости: природа происхождения // Вестник ЧелГУ. 2017. №11 (407). URL: https://cyberleninka.ru/article/n/feykovye-novosti-priroda-proishozhdeniya

42. Раҳимова Ш. Ёшларда ахборот алмашинуви маданиятини ривожлантириш истиқболлари. Infolib, №1, 2020 ахборот-кутубхона журнали //https://einfolib.uz/.

43. РепортажДаниилаТуровского//Медуза.2016. 15августа.URL:https://meduza.io/feature/2016/08/15/zashifrovannoe-podpolie.

44. Смирнов А. «Глубокие фейки»: сущность и оценка потенциального влияния на национальную безопасность // Свободная мысль. 2019. № 5.

45. Серов А. Дезинформация как инструмент внешней политики ряда зарубежных стран // Зарубежное военное обозрение. 2019. № 8.

46. Суходолов А. П. Феномен «фейковых новостей» в современном медиапространстве // Евроазиатское сотрудничество, гуманитарные аспекты: Материалы Международной конф. Иркутск: Изд-во Байкальского гос. ун-та, 2017.

47. Тихонова М. Стратегия противодействия распространению ложных новостей в социальных сетях. ВКР. Москва 2019. //www. allbestru/.

48 Трудоустройство в Финнляндии в 2022 году: на какую зарплату можно рассчитывать?//ttps://zagranportal.ru/finliandia/rabota/

49. Тулеубекова А. Н.-С. Почти 200 фейков о коронавирусе зафиксировали Международные организации [Электронный ресурс] // Сетевое издание "Zakon.kz". URL: https://www.zakon.kz/5005826-pochti-200-feykov-o-koronaviruse.html дата обращения: 20.06.2020.

50. Тулеубекова А. Н.-С. Ряд пользователей соцсетей арестованы за распространение фэйков про коронавирус [Электронный ресурс] // Там же. URL: https://www.zakon.kz/5006009-ryad-polzovateley-sotssetey-arestovany.html

51. Финляндия қандай қилиб дунёдаги энг яхши таълим тизимига эга бўлди?// https://zamin.uz/dunyo/ 2014-2022 «Zamin» - Ўзбекистон янгиликлари.

52. Финляндия қандай қилиб дунёдаги энг яхши таълим тизимига эга бўлди? https://zamin.uz/dunyo 14.02.2020

53. Хлызова Н.Ю. Средства массовой информации и средства массовой коммуникации как сновные понятия медиаобразования/ Под ред. Л.П. Громовой. [Текст]/ СПб., 2008.

54. Фальшивые новости и эпоха постправды: всё только начинается [Электронный ресурс] URL https://habr.com/post/399431

55. Фатеева И.А. Медиаобразование: теоретические основы и опыт реализации. Челябинск: Изд-во Челяб. гос. ун-та, 2007.

56. Федоров А.В. Медиаобразование и медиаграмотность. Таганрог: Изд-во Кучма, 2004.

57. Что такое фейковые новости и как за них будут наказывать? [Электронный ресурс] // Официальный сайт Государственной Думы РФ. URL: http://duma.gov.ru/news/29982/

58. Шанхайская конвенция о борьбе с терроризмом, сепаратизмом и экстремизмом. Шанхай, 15 июня 2001 г. Ратифицирована Постановлением ОМРУз от 30 августа 2001 года N 274-II https://nrm.uz/contentf?doc=51369

59. Экстремизм в сети Интернет: как не попасть в ловушку. // https://ntstiso.ru/wp-content/uploads/2021/05/.

60. Экстремизмга қарши курашиш тўғрисида" Ўзбекистон Республикаси қонуни.// qarash.uz.

61. Attkisson Sharyl. The Smear: How Shady Political Operatives and Fake News Control What You See, What You Think, and How You Vote. HarperCollins, 2017

62. Collins. Free Online Dictionary. [Электронный ресурс] URL https://www.collinsdictionary.com/woty.

63. DiMaX. «Фейк» хабарларга қарши курашиш нега муҳим?// "Terabayt.Uz" ахборот технологиялари сайти

64. Fake news is very real word of the year for 2017 // The Guardian. 2017. November 2. URL: https:/www.theguardian.com/books/2017/nov/02

65. Kaminska, Izabella (January 17, 2017). "A lesson in fake news from the info-wars of ancient Rome". Financial Times. Financial Times. Retrieved July 4, 2017.

66. Kubey, R. (1998). Obstacles to the Development of Media Education in the United States. Journal of Communication (Winter), pp.58-69

65. Makovich G.V. Communicative technologies in professional group activities [Электронный ресурс] // Management Issues. 2019. № 03 (58). URL: http://vestnik.uapa.ru/en/issue/2014/03/21.

67. Remove, Reduce, Inform: New Steps to Manage Problematic Content. [Электронный ресурс: https://newsroom.fb.com/news/2019/04/remove-reduce-inform-new-steps/]

68. Fazio, Lisa K.,Brashier, Nadia M.,Payne, B. Keith,Marsh, Elizabeth J. Knowledge does not protect against illusory truth. Journal of Experimental Psychology: General, Vol 144(5), Oct 2015, 993-1002 URL https://apa.org/pubs/journals/features/xge-0000098.pdf.

69. Pedro G. Lind, Luciano R. da Silva, José S. Andrade, Jr., and Hans J. Herrmann. Phys. Rev. E 76, 036117 – Published 27 September 2007 URL https://proxylibrary.hse.ru:2291/pre/abstract/10.1103/PhysRevE.76.036117 .

70. Rubin V. Deception Detection and Rumor Debunking for Social Media. The SAGE Handbook of Social Media Research Methods, Chapter: Deception Detection and Rumor Debunking for Social Media, Publisher: Sage, Editors: Luke Sloan, Anabel Quan-Haase.2017.

71. Soroush Vosoughi, Deb Roy and Sinan Aral. The spread of true and false news online.Science.[Электронныйресурс:https://science.sciencemag.org/content/359/6380/1146/tab-pdf]

72. Word of the Year 2016 is... [Electronic resource]. URL: https://en.oxforddictionaries.com/word-of-the-year/word-of-the-year-2016

73. UNESKO Recommendations Addressed to the United Nations Educational Scientific and Cultural Organization UNESCO. In Education for the Media and the Digital Age Vienna.1999.

74. UNESCO,. Media education. Paris: UNESCO.1984.

4. Printed and electronic mass media

1. Allcott H. social media and fake news in the 2016 election [Elektronnыy resurs] / National Bureau Econimic Research; H. Allcott, M. Gentzkow. R. 1187. – Rejim dostupa: dostupa: http://www.nber.org/papers.

2. Allcott H., Gentzkow M. (2017) Social Media and Fake News in the 2016 Election. Journal of Economic Perspectives. Vol. 31. No. 2. P. 222. https://doi.org/10.1257/jep.31.2.211.

3. Alimov.B. Ikkisidan birini tanlang: pandemiyami yoki infodemiya?. http://beruniyalimov.uz/archives/896

4. Brummette J., DiStaso M., Vafeiadis M., Messner M. (2018) Read All About It: The Politicization of "Fake News" on Twitter. Journalism & Mass Communication Quarterly. Vol. 95. No. 2. https://doi.org/10.1177/1077699018769906.

5. Bovet A., Makse H. A. (2019) Influence of Fake News in Twitter during the 2016 US Presidential Election. Nature Communications. Vol. 10. https://doi.org/10.1038/s41467-018-07761-2.

6. Borden S.L., Tew C. (2007). The role of journalist and the performance of journalism: Ethical lessons from «fake» news (seriously) // Journal of Mass Media Ethics. Vol. 22. №. 4.

7. Blair S., Busam J. A., Forstner S., Glance J., Green G., Kawata A., Kovvuri A., Martin J., Morgan E., Sandhu M., Sang R., Scholz-Bright R., Welch A. T.,

Wolff A. G., Zhou A., Nyhan B. (2019) Real Solutions for Fake News? Measuring the Effectiveness of General Warnings and Fact-Check Tags in Reducing Belief in False Stories on Social Media. Political Behavior. P. 12. https://doi.org/10.1007/s11109-019-09533-0.

8. De Vreese, C.H. (2020). News framing: Theory and typology. Information Design Journal + Document Design 13(1).

9. Entman, R. B. Framing: Toward clarification of a fractured paradigm. Journal of Communication. (2017).

10. Friggeri A., Rumor Cascades [Elektronny resurs] / Proceedings of the Eighth International AAAI Conference on Weblogs and Social Media; A. Friggeri, L. A. Adamic, D. Eckles, J. Cheng. - R.

11. Fact checking in the 2019 election: research recommendations https://www.google.com/url?client=internal-element.

12. Hallahan, K. (2019). Seven models of framing: Implications for public relations. Journal of Public Relations Research, 11(3).

13. Kubey, R. (1998). Obstacles to the Development of Media Education in the United States. Journal of Communication (Winter).

14. Media Literacy: A Report of the National Leadership Conference on Media Literacy. Queenstown, MD: The Aspen Institute.

15. Messing de Witte M. (2020) How to Avoid COVID-19 Fake News. Nextgov. March 19th. URL: https://www.nextgov.com/ ideas/2020/03/how-avoid-covid-19-fake-news/163904/

16. Назаров М. М. Международный опыт борьбы с фейками. На кого равняется Россия - Рамблер/новости (rambler.ru) .

17. Пулатова С.Р. Психосемантика ментальности: коммуникативный аспект // Проблемы медиапсихологии. Материалы сексии «Медиапсихология» Международной научно-практической конференции «Журналистика в ХХИ

веке: реалии и прогнозы развития», Москва, МГУ, 2021.

18. Qosimova N. "Mediaekologiya: axborot muhitining sofligi masalalari". T-2017. N2 "O'zbekiston xorijiy tillar jurnali.

19. Разлогов К.Э. Что такое медиаобразование?//Медиаобразование. 2005. № 2.

20. Creech B., Roessner A. (2019) Declaring the Value of Truth: Progressive-Era Lessons for Combatting Fake News. Journalism Practice. Vol. 13. No. 3. https://doi.org/10.1080/17512786.2018.1472526.

21. Samisov O.,Hayitova L., Abduvaliyev A., Norbo'tayev F., Mamarasulov U., Ermatov A.O'zbekistonda matbuot do'konlari nega kamaymoqda? Gazeta va jurnallarga talabning pasayishida do'konlarning "ayb"i kattami? [internet nashri] 21.01.2022.

22. Cappello G., Felini D., Hobbs R. (2011) Reflections on Global Developments in Media Literacy Education: Bridging Theory and Practice. Journal of Media Literacy Education 3(2).

23. Сатторов Б.Д. К определению понятий «текст» и «медиатекст» // Вестник Московского университета. Серия 10. Журналистика. 2020. № 2.

24. Scheufele, D, A, (2019), Framing as a theory of media effects, Journal of Communication, 49(1).

25. Clayton K., Blair S., Busam J. A., Forstner S., Glance J., Green G., Kawata A., Kovvuri A., Martin J., Morgan E., Sandhu M., Sang R., Scholz-Bright R., Welch A. T., Wolff A. G., Zhou A., Nyhan B. (2019) Real Solutions for Fake News? Measuring the Effectiveness of General Warnings and Fact-Check Tags in Reducing Belief in False Stories on Social Media. Political Behavior. P. 13. https://doi.org/10.1007/s11109-019-09533-0.

26. Creech B., Roessner A. (2019) Declaring the Value of Truth: Progressive-Era Lessons for Combatting Fake News. Journalism Practice. Vol. 13. No. 3. P. 263—279. https:// doi.org/10.1080/17512786.2018.1472526.

27. Вартанова Е. Л. К вопросу об актуализации теории журналистики и теории СМИ / Е. Л. Вартанова

// Вопросы теории и практики журналистики. — 2017. — Т. 6, № 1.— ДОИ: 10.17150/2308-6203.2017.6(1).5-13.

28. Zengerle P. (2016) Clinton Calls "Fake News" a Threat to U. S. Democracy. Reuters. December 9th. URL: https://www. reuters.com/artlcle/us-usa-cllnton-fakenews-ldUSKBN 13X2R6.

29. Шариков, А. В. Так что же такое медиаобразование? [Текст] / А. В. Шариков // Медиаобразование. — 2005. — № 2.

5. Websites

1. Moʻminova G. Emlash 95 foiz boʻlgan mamlakatda epidemiya tarqalishi kulgili // "Zarnews.uz"(13.08.2019 16:09).
2. iPhone 14 Pro sotib olish uchun buyragini sotayotganlar.https://www.xabar.uz/xorij/iphone-14-pro-sotib-olish-uchun https://daryo.uz/2022/01/31/ijtimoiy-tarmoq-va-messenjerlardan-qancha-ozbekistonlik-foydalanishi-malum-qilindi/
3. https://expandedramblings.com/index.php/fake-news-statistics/
4. https://ru.wiktionary.org/wiki/%D1%84%D0%B5%D0%B9%D0%BA www.advesti.ru/glossary/desk/19521
5. United Nations Human Rights Declaration, Article 19 (1948). http://www.un.org/en/documents/udhr/index.shtml
6. Internet World Stats: www.internetworldstats.com
7. clemi.fr
8. constitution.uz
9. csec.uz
10. davr24.uz
11. en.unesco.org

12. kh-davron.uz
13. kukaldosh.uz
14. kun.uz
15. lex.uz
16. medialit.org.
17. newreporter.org
18. old.muslim.uz
19. rsf.org
20. stat.uz
21. theguardian.com
22. uza.uz
23. xs.uz

www.ingramcontent.com/pod-product-compliance
Lightning Source LLC
LaVergne TN
LVHW010344070526
838199LV00065B/5786